Reproductive Medicine and the Law

Reproductive Medicine and the Law

Edited by

A. Allan Templeton
Professor of Obstetrics and Gynaecology,
University of Aberdeen, UK

Douglas J. Cusine
Senior Lecturer,
Department of Conveyancing and Professional Practice of Law,
University of Aberdeen, UK

CHURCHILL LIVINGSTONE
EDINBURGH LONDON MELBOURNE AND NEW YORK 1990

CHURCHILL LIVINGSTONE
Medical Division of Longman Group UK Limited

Distributed in the United States of America by Churchill
Livingstone Inc., 1560 Broadway, New York, NY
10036, and by associated companies, branches and
representatives throughout the world.

© Longman Group UK Limited 1990

First published 1990

ISBN 0 443 044104

British Library Cataloguing in Publication Data
Reproductive medicine and the law.
  1. Great Britain.   Man.   Reproduction.   Scientific
innovation.   Legal aspects
  I. Templeton, A. Allan   II. Cusine, D. J. (Douglas
James) *1946–*
344.104419

Library of Congress Cataloging-in-Publication Data
Reproductive medicine and the law/edited by A. Allan
  Templeton, D. Cusine.
      p. cm.
  Consists primarily of papers from a conference held at the
University of Aberdeen in 1989.
  Includes index.
  ISBN 0-443-04410-4
  1. Human reproductive technology—Government policy
—Great Britain—Congresses.   2. Human reproduction
—Law and legislation—Great Britain—Congresses.
3. Medical ethics—Great Britain—Congresses.
4. Medical ethics—Great Britain—Congresses.
  I. Templeton, A. A. (Alexander Allan)   II. Cusine,
Douglas J.
  [DNLM: 1. Ethics, Medical—Great Britain—
congresses.   2. Reproduction—Great Britain—
legislation—congresses.   3. Reproduction Technics—
Great Britain—legislation—congresses.
WQ 33 FA1 R4 1989]
RG133.5.R464   1990
176—dc20
DNLM/DLC
for Library of Congress   90-2039
                                                 CIP

Printed and bound in Great Britain by
Butler & Tanner Ltd, Frome and London

Preface

Having worked together for many years on various medical, legal and ethical issues raised by reproduction and reproductive techniques, we thought it desirable to create a forum in Aberdeen for such discussions. We persuaded the University to institute an annual Medico-legal lecture and we decided that, at least for the first such lecture, we should make it the culmination of a day conference. This book is the product of that conference.

We were fortunate to receive an enthusiastic response from all our speakers and chairmen. They are distinguished in their various fields and we are grateful to them for their contributions and support. We were impressed how the main discussants led the discussion and brought the main points together for this publication.

The conference would not have been a success without an attentive and informed audience and many came from all parts of the UK to make a very successful day.

The topics covered in the book are all of those which were discussed on the day, but three papers have been added on the subject of AIDS. We were convinced that the conference would be more useful if we concentrated on only a few topics as that would allow full presentations by the speakers and adequate opportunity for discussion. The quality of the papers and the discussion leaves us in no doubt that we were right.

Of those who spoke, we should perhaps mention two people in particular. One is Gordon Dunstan who had the difficult task of drawing together in a coherent way the themes of the day and to present them in some meaningful way. This he did with his accustomed skill. The Medico-legal lecture was given by Dame Mary Donaldson. It is always somewhat daunting to be the final speaker of the day, but Dame Mary's contribution was clear, considered and thought-provoking. To someone who said she had never given a lecture before, we offer our deepest thanks.

The conference was generously supported by the Medical and Dental Defence Union of Scotland and Ian Simpson's interest and enthusiasm are much appreciated.

Elaine Stirton not only did almost all of the preparatory work for the conference, but helped on the day to record the proceedings and answer and deal with any questions and problems. That in itself was of enormous value to us, but in addition, she took on the responsibility of ensuring that the conference papers were prepared for publication. To her we offer our gratitude.

Churchill Livingstone, the publisher, are in our debt for agreeing to publish the proceedings. This is a challenge because the topics in the book change with amazing rapidity.

Once again, we wish to thank all who were involved in the conference and who have contributed to its success. We hope that this publication can now extend the proceedings to a wider audience.

Aberdeen, 1990

A.A.T.
D.J.C.

Contributors

David Baird
Department of Reproductive Biology, University of Edinburgh, Chalmers Street, Edinburgh

Rev. Kenneth M. Boyd
Honorary Fellow, Faculty of Medicine, University of Edinburgh; and Scottish Director, Institute of Medical Ethics

Alistair Cameron QC
Vice-Dean, Faculty of Advocates, Advocates Library, Parliament House, Edinburgh

Douglas Cusine
Senior Lecturer, Department of Conveyancing, University of Aberdeen, Aberdeen

Dame Mary Donaldson
123 Shakespeare Tower, Barbican, London, EC2Y 8DR

Gordon R. Dunstan
9 Maryfield Avenue, Pennsylvania, Exeter, EX4 6JN

Peter Howie
Department of Obstetrics & Gynaecology, University of Dundee Medical School, Ninewells Hospital, Dundee

Frank D. Johnstone
Senior Lecturer in Obstetrics & Gynaecology, Centre for Reproductive Biology, University of Edinburgh, Edinburgh

Alexander McCall-Smith
Faculty of Law, Old College, South Bridge, Edinburgh

Sheila A. M. McLean
Department of Forensic Medicine, University of Glasgow, Glasgow

Sir Malcolm Macnaughton
Department of Obstetrics & Gynaecology, Royal Infirmary, (Muirhead Professor of Obstetrics & Gynaecology, University of Glasgow), Glasgow

Derek Morgan
Fellow in Health Care, Centre for Philosophy & Health Care, University College, Swansea

Kenneth Norrie
Lecturer in Law, University of Aberdeen, Aberdeen

Zelda Pickup
Department of Law, Manchester Polytechnic, Manchester

E. Malcolm Symonds
Department of Obstetrics & Gynaecology, University Hospital, Queen's Medical Centre, Nottingham

A. Allan Templeton
Department of Obstetrics & Gynaecology, University of Aberdeen, Maternity Hospital, Aberdeen

Joyce Watson
Medical and Dental Defence Union of Scotland, Glasgow

Contents

Contraception or abortion

1. Post coital contraception and menstrual induction

D. T. Baird

The necessity for effective means of regulating human fertility is almost universally recognised by most responsible authorities. In a world with finite resources there inevitably comes a time when the demand, due to increasing pressure of population, exceeds the available supplies of essentials. For the individual the ability to control one's own fertility can be regarded as a basic human right. The deleterious effect of repeated childbearing on the health of women and children has been repeatedly demonstrated.

In the last 50 years there have been significant advances in methods of contraception which are both effective and relatively free from side-effects. Among these, the demonstration by Pincus and Chang that orally active synthetic gestagens would block ovulation and the subsequent development of the oral contraceptive pill has been a landmark in contraception[1]. 'Contraception' was coined as a convenient shortening of contra conception and virtually all existing methods of birth control act before fertilisation of the egg. However, because not all methods of contraception are fully effective and totally free from side-effects there is a need for alternatives which could prevent the establishment or continuation of pregnancy. These methods are not a substitute for the present established methods of fertility regulation; rather they complement these methods so that a wide range of contraceptive techniques are available to meet the differing needs of individual women as well as acting as a back up for contraceptive failure.

In this paper I shall consider the current methods of post coital contraception and menstrual induction as well as likely developments.

POST COITAL CONTRACEPTION

Unwanted pregnancies arise out of unpremeditated, occasional acts of unprotected intercourse, often deeply regretted[2]. There are now available a range of post coital agents which can be used to prevent the establishment of pregnancy. Reliable data on efficacy is difficult to obtain because the risk of pregnancy following intercourse even around the time of presumed ovulation is low (probably not greater than 25 per cent) but most published

3

series quote a pregnancy rate per exposed cycle of around 1 per cent. The mechanism by which post coital steroids inhibit pregnancy is unclear; they probably disrupt either tubal transport of the embryo and/or prevent its implantation in the uterus. All the present methods involving steroids are associated with a high incidence of side-effects i.e. nausea, vomiting and disturbance in menstrual pattern such that they are unsuitable for repeated use as a regular form of contraception. A further disadvantage is that with the exception of intrauterine devices they are ineffective if given more than 72 hours after ovulation and, hence, are unsuitable to be given late in the luteal phase around the time of the expected next menstrual period to induce menstruation.

'ONCE A MONTH' PILL

The present oral contraceptive pills are highly effective means of avoiding conception but are not totally free from side-effects. Moreover, the pills must be taken for at least three out of four weeks prophylactically and, hence, on many occasions when there has been no risk of pregnancy. There would be considerable advantages in a pill which could be taken around the day of expected menses which would prevent or disrupt the process of implantation. If the administration were delayed until the period was two or three days overdue, the pill would probably need only be taken two or three times per year, even if a couple have frequent regular intercourse. Because a pill administered in this way would not prevent conception it has been suggested that the term 'contragestion' be used to embrace methods of fertility regulation which act by preventing or disrupting implantation and causing early abortion.

A promising recent development has been the synthesis of steroids with antigestagenic properties[3]. In all mammals the secretion of progesterone by the corpus luteum is essential to create a favourable environment for the nourishment of the developing embryo and its subsequent implantation in the uterus. Mifepristone (RU 486) is a synthetic steroid structurally related to norethindrone but which binds to gestagenic and glucocorticoid receptors but fails to initiate the changes in the synthesis of RNA which are essential for the mediation of hormone action. By occupying the receptor for progesterone on the uterus, it blocks the action of progesterone and, hence, prevents pregnancy.

Although the majority of women experience bleeding after taking mifepristone in the late luteal phase of the cycle, preliminary studies suggest that pregnancy is interrupted in only about 85 per cent of cases. Thus with the present regime the failure rate is too high to be used as a regular 'once a month' pill to be used only when there was a risk of pregnancy.

Even if a highly effective 'once a month' pill was to be developed, there may be ethical and legal constraints to its use. Such a pill would not stop fertilisation and would only prevent pregnancy by disrupting the implanting or recently implanted embryo. In a preliminary survey conducted in Edinburgh, only 50 per cent of a small sample of women attending a Family Planning Clinic reported that they would find such a method acceptable ethically as a regular form of contraception[4]. In those who accepted the method in principle, the vast majority said they would prefer to take the pill only when the period was overdue rather than at the time of the missed menstrual period. Presumably, the advantage of only taking the pill when pregnancy was presumed, outweighed the disadvantage of a greater certainty of inducing an early abortion.

However, the legal position of such a method of contragestion is unclear. In the UK, the Department of Health ruled that post coital steroids and intrauterine devices are considered as contraceptives and not as abortifacients[5]. A 'once a month' pill given before or at the time of the period could be considered as a late post coital agent even although it would be feasible using very sensitive assays for hCG to determine with reasonable certainty as to whether an embryo was inplanting in the uterus. The legal status of a pill given two or three days after the missed menstrual period may differ depending on the legal code of the country and is discussed further in the next chapter.

MENSTRUAL INDUCTION

All methods of contraception have a failure rate related either to the method itself or its use. Thus, in the foreseeable future it is likely that methods of inducing abortion will remain necessary to prevent the birth of unwanted children. Until very recently the only means of inducing abortion were surgical, mainly involving evacuation of the uterus by vacuum aspiration. In very early pregnancy (less than eight weeks amenorrhoea from the last menstrual period or six weeks conception) the embryo is small enough (up to 20 mm) that the uterus can be evacuated by suction without prior dilatation of the cervix, often under local anaesthesia as an out-patient procedure. Although it is possible to confirm the presence of an embryo and placenta by determination of hCG and ultrasound examination, the woman may show no signs or symptoms of pregnancy and may only suspect pregnancy by the period of amenorrhoea. Termination of pregnancy at this stage is often termed 'menstrual induction' and is associated with minimal complications.

Many pregnancies abort spontaneously at this time and the products of conception are passed without the necessity for surgical evacuation. Over the last 20 years research has concentrated on the development of compounds which could induce abortion medically at this stage of pregnancy. Such an approach has many advantages not the least of which is that it would make abortion more accessible, safer and potentially cheaper in those developing countries in which medical facilities and surgical skills are in short supply.

It was shown nearly 20 years ago by Karim and Filshie that PGE_2 and $PGF_{2\alpha}$ would induce abortion successfully in early pregnancy if injected into the uterus[6]. These natural prostaglandins are rather unstable and require to be injected into the uterus to be effective. Since then several relatively stable analogues of prostaglandins have been developed which will induce abortion when given by intramuscular injection (e.g. sulprostone) or by vaginal pessary (e.g. gemeprost)[7]. These compounds have been tested widely and been shown in comparative trials to be as effective as vacuum aspiration in pregnancies up to eight weeks amenorrhoea. Unfortunately, the dose required to induce abortion in over 90 per cent of women is associated with pain, diarrhoea and vomiting in 20–40 per cent of women. Thus, although prostaglandins are a safe, effective alternative to vacuum aspiration of the uterus, the high incidence of side-effects makes it unlikely that they will be acceptable to the majority of women.

The discovery of antiprogestational compounds, particularly those that act by blocking the progesterone receptor, represent without doubt the most significant development in hormonal regulation of fertility since the introduction of the combined contraceptive pill[8]. By antagonising the effect of progesterone on the uterus e.g. mifepristone, or inhibiting its synthesis e.g. epostane, endogenous prostaglandins are released, bleeding from the decidua occurs and abortion is induced. The initial publication reported that of 11 pregnant women (6–8 weeks amenorrhoea) given mifepristone by mouth, eight aborted completely, one required emergency evacuation of the uterus to control heavy bleeding and in two women the pregnancy continued[9]. Subsequently, extensive investigations using a range of doses have confirmed these initial findings that after taking mifepristone alone, 15–40 per cent of women fail to abort completely[3]. The failure rate appears to be higher the greater the period of amenorrhoea but even in very early pregnancy (less than 38 days amenorrhoea) the failure rate (15 per cent) is too high to be clinically useful.

The reason why some women fail to abort completely following anti-gestagens is unknown. It does not appear to be related to a variation in the dose or in the level of mifepristone in blood. Some bleeding almost always is provoked following mifepristone even in those women in whom the pregnancy continues. The mechanism by which mifepristone induces bleeding and abortion is not yet clear although it is probably related to the release of prostaglandins by the decidua and fetal membranes. There is a progressive increase in the sensitivity of the uterus to exogenous prosta-glandins following mifepristone and it was this observation which led to the therapeutic trial of mifepristone in combination with prostaglandin[10]. When mifepristone was followed 36 to 48 hours later by a small dose of sulprostone or gemeprost, 95 per cent of women aborted completely [10,11,12]. Moreover, because the dose of prostaglandin used is less than one-fifth of that required to induce complete abortion when used on its own, the incidence of pain, diarrhoea and vomiting is much reduced.

Subsequently, extensive trials have confirmed these initial observations that 'combination therapy' is a highly effective means of inducing abortion medically in early pregnancy. Although the optimum dose and timing of mifepristone and prostaglandin is not yet known, it has been demonstrated that a single 600 mg oral dose of mifepristone followed 48 hours later by 1 mg gemeprost vaginal pessary or 0.25 mg sulprostone intramuscularly, will induce abortion in over 95 per cent of pregnant women of less than eight weeks amenorrhoea. Following abortion the vaginal bleeding continues for approximately 10 days and in some (about 4 per cent) it may be necessary to evacuate the uterus surgically because of retained products of conception. In about 1 per cent of women, surgical evacuation may be necessary at the time of expulsion of the embryo because of heavy bleeding.

Following abortion, bleeding continues for about 10 days although the amount and duration varies considerably among individual women. In one series in which blood loss was measured objectively, the range was 14–512 ml with the median (74 ml) being equivalent to a heavy period[13]. The incidence of post-abortion infection appears to be similar to that of surgical termination at this gestation.

In summary, although the optimum regime of treatment has not yet been determined, the present combination therapy of a single 600 mg dose of mifepristone followed 48 hours later by 1 mg gemeprost vaginal pessary or 0.25–0.5 mg sulprostone by intramuscular injection is a highly effective and safe method of medical termination of pregnancy under eight weeks amenorrhoea. What medical, legal and/or ethical issues does this novel treatment present?

Legal and ethical aspects of menstrual induction

The current combination of antigestagen and prostaglandin is highly effective but like surgical termination is not 100 per cent effective. Three to five per cent of women will have continued bleeding due to an incomplete abortion and may require surgical evacuation of the uterus. With refinement of the timing and the dose of antigestagen and prostaglandin the need for surgical intervention will probably decrease. Indeed clinical trials have shown that as investigators become more familiar with medical induction of abortion, the incidence of surgical evacuation for incomplete abortion decreases. It seems likely, however, that a small number of women (probably about 1 per cent) will bleed heavily and require some form of haemostatic procedure. For this reason it is advisable that there is ready access to a trained gynaecologist. Although this does not mean that all medical abortions should be carried out necessarily in a hospital, it will inevitably constrain the extent to which this method of induction of abortion is available.

Apart from the medical considerations, there are legal consequences which are likely to vary depending on individual countries. In the UK the 1967 Abortion Act requires that two registered medical practitioners state in good faith that, in their opinion, there are grounds for termination. In addition, the treatment must be given in a National Health Service hospital or in registered premises licensed for this purpose by the Secretary of State. At present, licences are only granted to those premises which meet certain criteria having available facilities for resuscitation, giving of anaesthetic etc. Thus, although in the future additional premises may be licensed for medical abortions only, using less demanding criteria than for surgical abortions, the requirement for direct involvement of doctors will remain.

In addition to the concern about safety, there could be problems with controlling the distribution of such a potent compound. Antigestagens have the ability to induce bleeding and probable termination of the pregnancy at any stage of gestation. Preliminary data suggest that they markedly enhance the abortifacient efficacy of prostaglandins in mid-trimester pregnancy and mifepristone has been used to induce labour in late pregnancy in women carrying fetuses which are grossly abnormal or dead[14,15]. Because the risk of haemorrhage is probably greater in late pregnancy than in the first two months, it is obviously important that efforts should be made to prevent the taking of antigestagens in these circumstances except under strict medical supervision. A complex system of distribution has been used in France in which the makers Roussel UCLAF only supply the compound to pharmacies at clinics licensed to perform abortions. However, the compound is likely to have application in other areas of medicine such as endometriosis and breast cancer. When such uses become established medical practice the present cumbersome method of distribution will become impracticable.

It has been argued that the development of antigestagens for menstrual induction will make therapeutic abortion 'too easy' and encourage women to use abortion as a method of fertility regulation rather than contraception. This argument seems very unconvincing to me as few women appear to make the decision of choosing an abortion easy, by whatever means. It has also been argued that an extensive black market will develop increasing the number of illegal abortions. The present evidence suggests that the incidence of complications from abortion is lowest in those countries with liberal abortion laws. In countries where abortion is illegal or the laws very restrictive, there is a high incidence of illegal abortion. Because these abortions are often performed by unskilled people in less than adequate facilities, the rate of complications is high. It has been calculated by WHO that approximately 200 000 women per year die throughout the world as a result of complications of illegal abortions.

REFERENCES

1. Pincus G (1965) Control of Human Fertility. Academic Press, London & New York

2. Van Look P F A (1990) Post-coital contraception: A cover up story. In: Fertility Regulation Today and Tomorrow. Eds E Diczfalusy and M Bygdeman. Raven Press, New York. p 29–42
3. Bygdeman M & Van Look P F A (1988) Antiprogesterones for the interruption of pregnancy. Baillière's Clinical Obstetrics & Gynaecology 2: 617–630
4. Baird D T & Cameron I T (1985) Menstrual induction: surgery versus prostaglandins. In: Abortion: medical progress and social implications. Eds Ruth Porter & Maeve O'Connor. Ciba Foundation Symposium 1151, 178–186. Pitman, London
5. Havers M (1983) Hansard 42 (112) Columns 238–239
6. Karim S M M (1971) Once-a-month vaginal administration of prostaglandins E_2 and $F_{2\alpha}$ for fertility control. Contraception 3, 173
7. Bygdeman M & Green K K (1979) Menstrual Regulation: Medical Techniques. In: Pregnancy Termination: Procedures, Safety and New Developments. Eds G I Zatuchni, J J Sciarra & J J Spiedel. Harper & Row, p 69–77
8. Baulieu E E & Ulmann A (1986) Antiprogesterone activity of RU 486 and its contragestive and other applications. Human Reproduction 1, 107–110
9. Herrman W, Wyss R, Riondel A et al (1982) Effet d'un stéroide antiprogesterone chez la femme interruption du cycle menstrual et de la grossesse au début. C R Acad Sc. Paris, 294: 933–938
10. Bygdeman M & Swahn M-L (1985) Progesterone Receptor Blockage. Effect on uterine contractility and early pregnancy. Contraception 32, 45–51
11. Cameron I T, Michie A F & Baird D T (1986) Therapeutic Abortion in Early Pregnancy with Antigestagen RU 486 alone or in combination with prostaglandin analogue (Gemeprost). Contraception 35, 459–467
12. Baird D T, Rodger M W, Cameron I T & Roberts I (1988) Prostaglandins and antigestagens for the interruption of early pregnancy. J Reprod Fert Suppl. 36: 173–179
13. Rodger M W & Baird D T (1989) Blood loss following induction of eary abortion using mifepristone (RU 486) and a prostaglandin analogue (Gemeprost). Contraception 40, 439–447
14. Frydman R, Fernandez H, Pons J-C & Ulmann A (1988) Mifepristone (RU 486) and therapeutic late pregnancy termination: a double-blind study of two different doses. Human Reproduction 3, 803–806
15. Urquhart D R, Bahzad C & Templeton A A (1989) Efficacy of the antiprogestin mifepristone (RU 486) prior to prostaglandin termination of pregnancy. Human Reproduction 4, 202–203

2. Post coital anti-pregnancy techniques and the law

K. Norrie

INTRODUCTION

Family planning is aimed at the deliberate interruption of the process of human reproduction. That is a long and complex process and there are many points at which it can be interrupted. Traditional methods of family planning have been designed to take effect shortly before or during sexual intercourse, by preventing, in some way, a man's sperm from fertilising a woman's egg. So the cap and the condom prevent the two joining, as do the so-called natural methods such as the rhythm method and *coitus interruptus*. Other methods, such as the various forms of oral contraceptive pills, are designed to inhibit ovulation and so effectively make the woman's egg unavailable for fertilisation. But none of these methods is without problems. Some are not reliable; others have potentially serious side-effects. Consequently, the search has continued for new and better ways of interrupting the reproductive process, indeed has gathered momentum as family planning has become more accepted as a proper part of medical practice.

Researchers in the field of fertility control have relatively recently turned their attention to a later stage in the reproductive process and, instead of trying to interrupt that process before the egg and the sperm meet, have been examining ways of preventing the fertilised egg from implanting itself in the lining of the uterus. It would seem that the process of implantation is an unreliable, uncertain and really rather random business, with a large percentage of fertilised eggs *naturally* failing to implant. So theoretically to disrupt the process at a stage that is chancy in any case, ought to be easier than disruption at a more certain stage. Two very new birth control techniques are being developed on this basis: there already exist long established contraceptive methods that have this effect. The existing methods are the intra-uterine contraceptive device, the so-called morning after pill, and menstrual extraction. All of these methods prevent the fertilised egg from implanting into the uterus. The new methods are hormonal, being anti-progesterones, and anti-human chorionic gonadotrophin (hCG) vaccines.

Progesterone is a hormone produced by women that allows the lining of

11

the womb to take and hold a fertilised egg. Similarly, human chorionic gonadotrophin is a hormone produced by the early developing embryo which is essential to allow it to implant in the uterus. If the progesterone receptors in the lining of the womb could be blocked, the fertilised egg could not implant; if an anti-hCG vaccine could encourage the woman's body to mount a hostile immune reaction to hCG, the fertilised egg would be unable to implant. The anti-progesterone, RU 486, is already in clinical use in France, and WHO are currently funding research into the development of an anti-hCG vaccine[1].

But there is a legal problem. These methods are designed to bring about the failure of implantation, that is, the destruction of a fertilised egg, and it is argued by some that this amounts to a criminal offence. It cannot amount to homicide since that crime requires the existence of a living *breathing* human person in the full sense of that word. Some writers argue, more plausibly, that the destruction of a fertilised egg that is not yet implanted amounts to abortion[2], and thus legal only if the conditions in the Abortion Act 1967 are satisfied. Whether it does or not depends upon the nature of the crime of abortion. There is no statute in Scottish or English law defining what abortion actually is, and one must therefore try to identify the elements that any charge of unlawful abortion must contain. If the destruction of a fertilised egg lacks any of the essential elements, then it cannot be abortion.

THE NATURE OF ABORTION

Medical practitioners often use the phrase 'termination of pregnancy' as if it were synonymous with abortion. But this is not so. Normal delivery terminates a pregnancy, but it is not abortion; a doctor inducing labour is terminating a pregnancy, but it is not abortion. Abortion in the sense of the law requires something more. It requires the intention to destroy potential human life by the termination of a pregnancy. There are (at least) three essential elements: destruction, intention to destroy, and termination of pregnancy. Destruction is a purely factual matter and causes no real problems for the law (except in trying to define what a 'potential human life' is). Intention does cause problems, because it is often terribly difficult to prove (as will be seen shortly). The real difficulties for the law come about however when we try to define termination of pregnancy.

Before a pregnancy can be terminated, it must have commenced, and this raises the question of when does the law regard a pregnancy as having commenced. In this country, the law is silent on the question of when a pregnancy begins. Some legal systems contain statutory definitions of when human life itself begins. In the recent case of *Webster v. Reproductive Health Services*[3], the United States Supreme Court refused to hold unconstitutional a statute's preamble which declared that human life begins on conception (by which it meant fertilisation). However, the question of when human life begins as a matter of morality, or indeed biology, is not the same as the question of when pregnancy begins for the purposes of the law. Human life may—or may not—begin in a test-tube, but the mere existence of a fertilised egg in a test-tube does not make the woman who produced the egg pregnant. The important issue, in law, is when *pregnancy* begins. A number of legal systems contain statutory definitions of the commencement of pregnancy rather than the commencement of human life, and many define it to commence on the completion of implantation. So, for example, New Zealand's Contraception, Sterilisation and Abortion Act 1977 defines abortion as the destruction of 'an embryo or fetus *after implantation*'. Similar statutory provisions are found in the Dutch, West German, and Austrian legal systems[4].

There is no such statute in Scottish or English law. However, the British courts have traditionally accepted the medical profession's definitions of such things as death, live-birth, mental competency and maturity, and many other things besides; and one can safely predict that the courts will also accept the medical definition of when pregnancy begins. Medically speaking, pregnancy begins on implantation, that is the completion of the process whereby the fertilised egg attaches itself to the wall of the uterus[5]. It follows that any anti-pregnancy technique that prevents implantation does not terminate pregnancy, because there is no pregnancy, and therefore cannot be abortion.

PARTICULAR POST COITAL METHODS

We may now apply these principles to the types of birth control methods mentioned at the beginning of this paper, in order to see how the law regards them, and to examine the legal problems their use can give rise to.

IUD

Insofar as the IUD prevents implantation, there is no crime committed because, for the reasons already given, it does not result in the termination of pregnancy. On the other hand, the dislodging by an IUD of an implanted embryo may well be criminal abortion if it is inserted with that intent. But there is a difficulty in Scottish law, since criminal abortion cannot be charged unless the woman was and can be proved to be actually pregnant[6]. But if the IUD is inserted at such an early time that no-one can tell whether there has yet been implantation, any prosecution for abortion must fail for lack of proof. So it would follow that a medical practitioner could fit an IUD with impunity, in Scotland, for so long after intercourse as it remains impossible to establish the existence of a pregnancy.

English law is quite different, because the prosecutor in England does not have to prove the existence of pregnancy in order to bring a successful charge of unlawful abortion. Illogically, a person can be convicted of unlawful abortion in England even although the woman on whom the operation was performed was not pregnant[7]. However, in practice, the position in that jurisdiction is much the same as in Scotland, though achieved by a slightly different route. This is because, while an actual pregnancy need not be proved, the prosecutor does always have to prove that the accused in fact believed that a pregnancy did exist. This is shown in the case of *R. v. Price* (1967)[8]. Here a doctor inserted an IUD into a woman who was three and a half months pregnant, and she miscarried two days later. The woman had told the accused that she was pregnant and that she wanted an abortion, but he told her that he did not believe that she was pregnant, and that she could therefore be fitted with an IUD to protect her in the future. A police surgeon who saw the woman shortly before she miscarried gave evidence that, in his view, the woman was 'manifestly' pregnant. The charge of inducing miscarriage by use of an IUD was held relevant, and the accused was convicted. However, the conviction was quashed on appeal, because there was not sufficient corroboration that the doctor believed the woman to be pregnant at the time he acted. The Court of Appeal made it quite plain that belief in a pregnancy was essential before the prosecutor could prove intent to terminate the pregnancy.

Suspicion of pregnancy would not be enough to found a charge, for suspicion does not amount to knowledge or belief. The prosecutor has to satisfy the criminal standard of proof—'beyond reasonable doubt', and so would have to prove beyond reasonable doubt that the doctor actually believed the woman to be pregnant. If a doctor fits an IUD some days after an episode of unprotected mid-cycle sexual intercourse, she or he will undoubtedly be aware of the possibility of pregnancy existing, just as Dr Price was, but could have no *knowledge* or *belief* in the actuality of pregnancy. On the other hand, if an IUD is fitted some weeks later, when a pregnancy test could be carried out, knowledge and intent might be inferred, because the courts might easily hold wilful ignorance to be the equivalent of knowledge.

Therefore, in practice, the law of England is much nearer to the law of Scotland than might appear at first sight, for of course the most satisfactory way of proving that the doctor believed the woman to be pregnant is to show that she is in fact pregnant. So, in both jurisdictions, a criminal charge would be successful only if, for example, the doctor had fitted an IUD after receiving a positive result of a pregnancy test, or after deliberately failing to perform such a test for fear of the result. Without a pregnancy being proved in Scotland, or without belief in a pregnancy being proved in England, no charge could be brought for the insertion of an IUD.

Menstrual extraction

Menstrual extraction is a post coital procedure whereby the uterine contents are sucked out at around the time the woman would expect to begin menstruating. This may be done for genuinely therapeutic reasons, for example, to assist a woman who suffers from dysmenorrhoea, or it may be done for birth control reasons, that is to extract any fertilised or implanted egg that may have been brought into existence by an episode of unprotected intercourse.

A charge of unlawful abortion through the use of such procedures would suffer the same difficulties of proof as those just described for the IUD. But the doctor ought to act in good faith. If a woman asks for menstrual extraction because her period is late, this might be provided; but if it is requested specifically and solely because the woman has recently had unprotected sexual intercourse, then it is difficult to accept that this is provided in good faith to assist menstruation. If it is performed at a time when pregnancy, that is implantation, could easily be established, then the doctor's legal position is much more precarious: wilful ignorance equals knowledge, and the dislodging of an implanted egg with knowledge equals abortion.

'Morning after' pill

High doses of oestrogen taken within 72 hours of unprotected inter-course will prevent pregnancy. Since this method is effective only for 72 hours after intercourse, and pregnancy could never be established within so short a time, it follows that its use within that time can never amount to unlawful abortion.

Anti-progesterones and anti-hCG vaccines

The legality of both anti-progesterones and anti-hCG vaccines used as post coital but pre-implantation contraceptives is not in doubt, and the same principles would be applied as for other methods that prevent implantation of the fertilised egg. Their use to dislodge already implanted eggs would on the other hand amount to abortion, but, again, the doctor's intent and knowledge will prove crucial. Any action upon very early embryos would be undetectable because the very existence of the embryo cannot be established at least for a number of days after implantation. So, even if these methods did act upon very recently implanted embryos, this does not bring these methods into the abortion regime, because the existence of, or belief in, implantation could not be proved.

However, there is a difference between established post-fertilisation contraceptive methods and anti-progesterones like RU 486, because RU 486 can dislodge the implanted egg at a much later stage, i.e. at a stage long after implantation can in fact be detected. If the doctor who administers RU 486 is aware that the woman is pregnant, and it is administered with the intent to end that pregnancy, then there is no doubt that this would amount to abortion, just as late insertion of an IUD with that knowledge and intent would amount to abortion. As a consequence, the use of RU 486 after the doctor knows the woman is pregnant will be legal only insofar as the conditions in the Abortion Act 1967 are satisfied. Roussel, the creators and developers of this drug, accept this, and are marketing it as an abortifacient, rather than as a contraceptive.

The provision of RU 486 only on satisfaction of the conditions in the Abortion Act will obviate any potential legal problems, but it does not, of course, silence criticism of the use of the drug from the anti-abortion lobby. The evidence shows that anti-progesterones provide a safe and non-invasive method of early abortion, which does not involve either surgery or general anaesthesia or an overnight stay in hospital. The side-effects so far reported have been of a minimal and acceptable nature. The criticisms made by the anti-abortion lobby (who talk, for example, of chemical warfare against children) are, in my view, in themselves quite immoral, for this reason. The fact is that abortion is in some circumstances legal in this country, and so long as that remains so, doctors who perform abortion have an ethical duty to perform it by the safest and most effective means available. Some countries, such as Italy, actually make it a legal duty to provide abortion and other family planning services in the least hazardous way. So, when RU 486 becomes available in Italy, there will be a statutory duty on doctors to use that method rather than other more hazardous methods.

Even in this country, one can easily construct an argument to the effect that there is a legal as well as an ethical duty to use RU 486 where appropriate. To subject a patient to dangerous treatment when there is safe treatment available that is equally efficacious amounts to an intentional infliction of harm, which is a civil and a criminal assault. If a woman had cancer of the breast that was susceptible to radiotherapy treatment, and a surgeon cut her breast off because he was a member of the Green Party and radiotherapy was not to his liking, who can doubt that he has grievously injured the woman and ought to be punished? To deny RU 486 when it would work, and force women to undergo surgical abortions instead is equally unacceptable, both in medical ethics and in law.

The anti-abortion lobby, of course, hopes that to make abortions more dangerous will make people resort to them less. This completely underestimates the nature and the strength of the human sex-drive. And it is the same argument as that which says that, in order to encourage safer driving on the roads, we should prohibit the use of safety helmets, safety belts, and reinforced chassis.

The law has historically tried to protect women's health. Abortion was criminal largely because of the dangers the operation posed to women. Abortion was legalised in many countries when it was realised that women would resort to the most dangerous forms of back-street abortions. The law ought to continue to protect women's health, and so long as abortion remains legal this means making it as safe—i.e. providing it as early—as possible. For its effect on women's health, the development and marketing of RU 486 is the most significant event in birth control since the discovery of the contraceptive pill itself. All right thinking people, whether they approve of abortion or not, ought to welcome this development.

REFERENCES

1. Research in Human Reproduction, Biennial Report 1986–1987, WHO, Geneva 1988, pp. 177–198
2. Tunkel, Modern Anti-Pregnancy Techniques and the Criminal Law (1974) Crim. L.R. 461, and 'Abortion: How Early, How Late and How Legal?' (1979) 2 B.M.J. 253; Keown, 'Miscarriage: A Medico-Legal Analysis' (1984) Crim. L.R. 604
3. 106 L.Ed 2d. 410 (1989)
4. Cook & Dickens, 'International Developments in Abortion Laws; 1977–1988' (1988) 76 Am. J. Pub. Health 1305
5. See 'Post-Coital Contraception' (1983) 1 The Lancet 853; Tietze & Henshaw, Induced Abortion: A World Review, 1986, 6th edn Alan Guttmachar Institute, New York
6. *H.M. Adv. v. Anderson* 1928 J.C. 1, *H.M. Adv. v. Semple* 1937 J.C. 41
7. Offences Against the Person Act 1861, s. 58
8. [1968] 2 All E.R. 282

3. Discussion for section 1

A. McCall-Smith

One of the most persistent problems encountered in criminal law is that of
defining the precise scope of a legal prohibition. This is illustrated quite
clearly in the law of abortion in the United Kingdom, where a not very
satisfactorily-drafted statute regulates what is undoubtedly the most
morally controversial area of medical practice. (The very exclusivity of the
statutory abortion regime in Scotland has elsewhere been called into
question by Norrie, and others, with the result that we possibly have two
laws of abortion in the United Kingdom, a situation which was surely not
intended by the promoters of the original legislation.)

Any discussion of a subject as complex as this, does well to begin with a
basic proposition. The fundamental purpose of legislation on abortion is
the prohibition of those acts which are intended to prevent the birth of an
already-conceived child. This aim may be inspired by a variety of
rationales, but at the root of the legal prohibition of abortion in most
societies is the belief that the taking of human life is morally wrong, even if
that human life happens to be in incipient or undeveloped form. To achieve
this end, though, legal rules must be framed, whether by legislation or by
court decision, and it is at this point that the inadequacy of legal language is
revealed. In the law on abortion, a number of expressions have been used
which may have a clear enough everyday meaning, but which, on close
analysis, reveal areas of uncertainty. In particular, when science makes the
sort of strides outlined by Professor Baird, the inadequacy or vagueness of
legal language comes into clear focus. When is a woman pregnant? What is a
miscarriage? The layman may experience no difficulty in answering these
questions to his own satisfaction, but the lawyer and the philosopher may
not be so certain. In circumstances where there is no ambiguity—as where,
for example, a woman who is nine weeks pregnant undergoes a procedure
for the surgical extraction of her fetus—the Abortion Act is clearly, and
unambiguously, applicable. In other cases, and particularly those cases
where use is made of chemical substances, the issue of the bluntness of the
existing legal terms is very much highlighted.

Dr Norrie's analysis of the legal issues associated with the use of drugs to
prevent implantation or to promote the expulsion of the implanted embryo
takes us to the kernel of this problem of definition. If one takes the view that

19

pregnancy begins on conception (and prior to implantation), then doing anything to prevent implantation amounts to an attempt to terminate pregnancy. Such acts also amount to an attempted frustration of the aim of the law criminalising abortion—namely, the prohibition of attempts to stop the birth of an already-conceived child. The purpose for which a statute was enacted is not, however, the principal consideration in the application of that statute, particularly in the literal tradition of statutory interpretation. If a statute talks about 'miscarriage' or 'abortion', then it is the meaning of these terms which a court must attempt to elucidate.

Dr Norrie's espousal of the position that pregnancy begins on implantation was greeted with considerable interest by the participants. The significance claimed for implantation is that it marks the point at which the embryo becomes part of the mother's body. This gives meaning to the term 'miscarriage', which is important, in view of the use of that term in legislation. Yet for some of the participants, at least, implantation and the notion of 'becoming part of the mother's body' was a troublesome one. Bishop Conti saw a fundamental flaw in any attribution of moral significance to implantation, and asked how a fertilised ovum could become part of a mother's body when it had a life of its own? The point was also raised that, from the scientific point of view, the theory that a fertilised embryo only 'relates' to the mother in a significant way after implantation has occurred was open to doubt. (The fertilised embryo, it appears, exchanges complicated signals with the mother's body even before implantation.)

The merit of Norrie's position is that it identifies a particular point at which the legal prohibition against abortion can begin. But is the stage of implantation the correct point? Morally, implantation has some significance: the embryo embarks on an important stage of its development on implantation, which is therefore a *sine qua non* of development to full legal and moral personhood. Yet, is implantation any more morally significant than conception? If it is, it can only be because physical attachment carries with it certain obligations for the person upon whom the embryo then becomes more tangibly and inextricably dependent.

Implantation should be considered the point at which legal protection of the fetus begins provided that the terms currently used in the statutes make it sensible to take implantation as the 'starting point' or, that there is evidence that the law has always regarded implantation as being legally significant. Unfortunately, there is no firm answer to the first of these questions. There is no consensus as to whether a woman who has within her an unimplanted embryo may be said to be pregnant: for some, she will be while for others, pregnancy requires implantation, and, short of a ruling from a linguistic arbiter, arguments in favour of either interpretation may be equally cogently put. As to the question of the attitude traditionally taken by the law on this point, there was a sharp exchange of differing views between Mr Keown and Dr Norrie. Mr Keown argued that the law has always been taken to protect the fertilised ovum from the point of conception; Dr Norrie queried this, asking for authority, which is admittedly difficult to locate.

Even if implantation is taken as the beginning of the legal regime of protection for the embryo, the difficulty of determining when implantation has occurred exercised the minds of a number of participants. Dr Norrie deals very clearly with the problems which this throws up for the criminal law (in terms of the proving of pregnancy or an actual belief of pregnancy), and the doubt which is occasioned by these issues effectively means that caution should still be exercised in the use of the drugs in question. Doctors might comply with the provisions of the Abortion Act in prescribing these drugs, and therefore avoid any legal difficulties, or, alternatively, there might be legislation legitimising the use of such drugs outwith the framework of the current legal regime on abortion. The latter course would probably be simplest, and would remove all legal doubt. It would, however, be an extension of the existing provisions on abortion, and insofar as it would take us even further down the road of abortion on demand, it might be expected to attract considerable criticism from those who regard the current restrictions on abortion as being farcical in the extent of their non-observance. Perhaps the real question to be asked is this: once one allows liberal abortion (effectively on maternal demand during the earlier stages of pregnancy), does it thereafter make any real difference what is defined as an abortion if the ultimate end is the same (the non-birth of an infant)? The answer is that there is a difference, at least in terms of medical control. Chemical methods could allow women to terminate pregnancy outwith direct medical control, and legislators must now decide whether it wishes to endorse this or subject it to direct medical control through legislation.

Selective reduction of multiple pregnancy

4. Selective reduction—medical aspects

P. W. Howie

One of the consequences of the new treatments of human infertility has been a sharp rise in the incidence of multiple pregnancy. This can have particularly serious consequences when the multiple pregnancies are of high order causing a wide range of potential problems for both the mother and her babies. One of the proposed responses to the difficulty created by high order multiple pregnancies has been selective reduction, a new procedure which raises a number of legal and ethical problems. This paper presents and discusses the medical applications of this new and controversial procedure.

DEFINITIONS

Before discussing selective reduction it is important to define what is meant by the procedure. In some of the literature there has been confusion between the terms selective feticide, selective reduction and antenatal sex selection. All of these procedures involve the induction of fetal death and an element of selection but differ fundamentally in their indications, their legal status and their ethical consequences.

Selective reduction

Selective reduction is a procedure which is carried out during the first trimester when a high order multiple pregnancy of three or more is reduced, usually to twins. Selective reduction is carried out without knowledge of either the sex or the normality of the fetus. The purpose of selective reduction is to improve the chances of healthy survival in the remaining conceptuses and to reduce the hazards to the mother.

Selective feticide

Selective feticide is usually carried out in the second trimester of a twin pregnancy when one of the twins has been shown to have a serious congenital abnormality. The justification for the procedure is that it will prevent the birth of a seriously handicapped child and may also reduce the risks of a pre-term birth in the healthy remaining fetus.

Sex selection

Antenatal sex selection is usually performed in a singleton pregnancy after antenatal diagnostic tests have been carried out to determine the fetal sex. Pregnancy termination by conventional means is then carried out if the fetal sex is not that desired by the parents. In a small number of cases the sex selection may have been carried out to avoid the risks of a sex-linked congenital disorder but in most cases the procedure is performed to meet the social or cultural desires of the parents. This procedure is discussed later in this symposium.

INDICATIONS FOR SELECTIVE REDUCTION

Selective reduction has been proposed as a means of ameliorating the serious risks associated with high order multiple pregnancy. High order multiple pregnancy is usually defined as a pregnancy with four or more conceptuses although triplets lie in a grey area and may be included in high order multiple pregnancies. The incidence of high order multiple pregnancy has risen sharply in recent years, the majority resulting from induction of ovulation regimes which led to hyperstimulation of the ovary and multiple ovulations. A smaller number of high order multiple pregnancies have resulted from embryo transfer during in vitro fertilisation or multiple oocyte replacements associated with gamete intrafallopian transfer. It is also possible to have high order multiple pregnancy as a result of spontaneous conception although the number of such pregnancies will be extremely small.

RISKS FROM HIGH ORDER MULTIPLE PREGNANCY

Fetal mortality

There is limited information on the mortality associated with high order multiple pregnancy but a study of registered multiple births in England and Wales between 1975–1983 has been reported by Botting et al (1987) [1]. Compared with a perinatal mortality of 13.8/1000 live and stillbirths during this period for singleton pregnancies, perinatal mortality rose to over 219/1000 in quads and 416/1000 in sextuplets (Table 4.1). Even amongst those infants who were born alive the subsequent infant mortality rose from 11.7/1000 live births in singletons to 220/1000 in quads and 500/1000 in sextuplets. These figures do not include the fetal losses occurring before 28 weeks so that the overall prospects for survival in high order multiple pregnancies are extremely low. Without the use of selective pregnancy there has been no recorded survivor following an octuplet pregnancy[2].

High order multiple pregnancy usually ends in pre-term birth, the duration of pregnancy being related to the number of conceptuses. It is well established that babies of low birthweight who survive have a high

Table 4.1 Mortality from high order multiple pregnancy, England and Wales 1975–1983

	Perinatal mortality	Infant mortality
Singleton	13.8	11.7
Twins	63.2	52.9
Triplets	164.5	147.7
Quads	219.5	220.1
Quintuplets	200.0	200.0
Sextuplets	416.7	500.0
	/1000 live and stillbirths	/1000 live births

incidence of subsequent handicap. From a study in Dundee[3] which examined all births occurring between 20–28 weeks during the period 1980–1984, figures are shown in Table 4.2. Of the children born at this gestational age, 66% were stillborn and a further 17% died by the age of one month giving an overall mortality rate of 83%. Six per cent of the total group developed a serious handicap after surviving for one month after birth, leaving a total proportion of 11% of the original population who survived without evidence of handicap. The range of handicap includes cerebral palsy, blindness and mental retardation.

Maternal morbidity

Apart from the serious risks of mortality and morbidity to the fetus, there are also several serious potential problems for the mother. Hyperemesis (excessive vomiting) is common and apart from causing great misery may present serious risks to the mother. Hospital admission for intravenous fluid therapy will commonly be required. High blood pressure is a common complication in high order multiple pregnancy and when this is severe may lead to fits, cerebral haemorrhage or placental bleeding; all of these conditions pose a potential threat to the mother's life. The high order multiple pregnancy may be associated with hydramnios (an excessive accumulation of fluid within the uterus). This condition causes severe discomfort to the mother and may confine her to bed for prolonged periods. Hydramnios substantially increases the risk of pre-term delivery and its adverse con-

Table 4.2 Outcome of pre-term births before 28 weeks in Dundee 1980–1984[3]

Outcome	
Stillbirths	66%
Death in first month	17%
Survival with serious handicap	6%
Survival without handicap	11%
Total	100%

sequences. If the mother is confined to bed for a prolonged period, the risk of thrombosis in her leg or pelvic veins increases sharply; if a blood clot should form and detach itself from the veins in the lower part of the body the mother may suffer a pulmonary embolism (the passage of a blood clot to the lungs) which may endanger her life.

Delivery is nearly always by Caesarean section which, in the circumstances of a high order multiple pregnancy, will add to the already substantial risks from the conditions mentioned above.

Social problems

The arrival of several babies presents a number of problems to the parents. The babies may spend a prolonged period of time in the special care nursery causing considerable stress and making psychological adjustment difficult. The simultaneous arrival of so many children may create severe financial problems because of the demands placed on accommodation and other resources to look after the children. Not all parents are able to cope with the necessary adjustments, and separation and divorce are not uncommon consequences of the high order multiple pregnancy.

Community problems

The increase in the number of pre-term babies as a consequence of high order multiple births has produced serious strains upon the facilities for delivering neonatal intensive care[4]. Such care is both demanding and expensive and the requirements of the babies produced by assisted reproduction have to compete with those delivered pre-term after singleton pregnancies conceived normally. Because many children delivered from a high order multiple pregnancy will develop serious handicap this will place demand upon the resources available for long-term care.

The realities of these problems was illustrated by Hobbins[5] when he described the outcome of a case of quintuplets delivered at 27 weeks. One baby died aged 2 days, one was blind and had necrotising enterocolitis, one had hydrocephalus following a brain haemorrhage, one developed chronic lung disease as a consequence of premature birth and the fifth had seizures due to ischaemia (lack of oxygen to the brain) in the perinatal period. The cost of neonatal care to the family was $300 000.

PREVENTION OF HIGH ORDER MULTIPLE PREGNANCY

In view of the risks associated with high order multiple pregnancy, there is a clear obligation upon clinicians to do everything possible to limit their number by optimising clinical management. This will require the best use of measures to monitor ovulation induction programmes and to limit the number of embryo or oocyte replacements in line with the recommendations of the Voluntary Licensing Authority (now Interim Licensing Authority). Nevertheless, despite optimum clinical management, high order multiple pregnancies will inevitably occur from time to time and present the clinician with a dilemma of management.

MANAGEMENT OF HIGH ORDER MULTIPLE PREGNANCY

When faced with a high order multiple pregnancy the clinician, who may not necessarily be the same person as the one who induced the high order multiple pregnancy in the first place, is faced with a difficult choice[6]. The clinician can either recommend that the pregnancy be allowed to continue, the pregnancy be terminated completely, or that selective reduction be carried out.

Allowing pregnancy to continue

For many couples the only acceptable option may be to allow the pregnancy to continue. Nevertheless, the parents have to face the possibility of an adverse fetal or maternal outcome as discussed above. In many of the cases in which the pregnancy is allowed to continue, the parents may have to face either disappointment or distress. The solution of allowing the pregnancy to continue has the advantage that it creates no ethical or legal problems and spares the parents from the feeling of guilt which may arise from 'act of commission' which they find difficult to accept.

Pregnancy termination

The second option is to terminate the entire pregnancy. This solution has the advantages that it will avoid the risk of long term handicap in the offspring and will protect maternal health. On the other hand it frustrates the desires of the parents to have children and many of these parents will have already experienced a prolonged period of infertility. Because of the risks to both mother and fetus there will be no difficulty in justifying termination of the entire pregnancy under the 1967 Abortion Act. Nevertheless, many of the parents who opt for complete termination of pregnancy may experience grief and deprivation. In addition, the lives of all the conceptuses are lost, an option which many couples will find unacceptable.

Selective reduction

The option of selective reduction has been recommended as a compromise between the options of continuing with the pregnancy and complete termination. It has been argued that it may give the best chances of a healthy mother with surviving healthy baby(s)[7]. By reducing the high order multiple pregnancy usually to twins, many of the financial and social problems will be reduced to acceptable limits. Nevertheless, selective reduction raises many legal and ethical problems which will be discussed in the next paper and the long term consequences of the procedure are unknown.

METHODS OF SELECTIVE REDUCTION

The number of reports of selective reduction are limited, the main papers being those of Evans et al (1988)[2] who reported on four cases and Berkowitz et al (1988)[7] who described 12 cases. In both of these reports all of the pregnancies have resulted from ovulation induction.

In their paper, Berkowitz et al described two methods of carrying out selective reduction. The first method was transcervical aspiration in which an 8 mm suction catheter was introduced through the cervix without dilatation and the lowest sac(s) aspirated using a 50 ml syringe. In one of their cases, severe bleeding was provoked during this method and they abandoned this technique in favour of a transabdominal approach. In the transabdominal approach a 20 guage needle was introduced under ultrasound control into the thorax of the uppermost fetus. A dose of between 2–7 mmol KCl was introduced into the pericardial area sometimes with the addition of 5–10 ml of sterile water. If asystole (cessation of heart beats) was achieved for 60 seconds it was assumed that fetal death had probably been induced although in some cases it was found that that fetus had subsequently survived. The procedure was commonly carried out under the cover of antibiotics and maternal sedation.

In their series of 12 cases, Berkowitz et al[7] carried out selective reduction in 4 cases of triplets, 5 cases of quads, 1 case of quintuplets and 2 cases of sextuplets. The procedure was usually performed between 11 and 12 weeks gestation because they found that spontaneous reduction could occur before that time. In 4 of the 12 pregnancies, all of the conceptuses were lost. In addition to the one already described in which excessive bleeding occurred following transcervical aspiration, the transabdominal approach led to complete abortion in three further cases at 4 weeks, 7 weeks and 8 weeks, respectively, after the selective reduction.

In the remaining 8 pregnancies, all of which were reduced to twins, 15 surviving babies were delivered. In one of the pregnancies, intrauterine death at 22 weeks occurred in one of the twins although the other baby was delivered alive and survived in good health. All of the 15 babies who survived after selective reduction appeared to be alive and well after followup, the great majority being delivered after 34 weeks and of birthweights above 1500 g. Berkowitz et al[7] claimed that a survival rate of 15 babies from 49 conceptuses was similar to the number of survivors that would have been obtained from a non-intervention policy allowing natural outcome; they claimed however that the morbidity was much lower in the surviving children than would have been expected from a policy of non-intervention.

In the series described by Evans et al[2] healthy twins were delivered in 2 of the 4 pregnancies reported, fetal loss occurring in the remaining 2 pregnancies. Once again the surviving fetuses (2 of whom survived from an octuplet pregnancy) were alive and well at one year of follow-up. It is this claim that selective reduction leads to a greater number of healthy surviving babies that underpins the medical argument in its favour.

POTENTIAL PROBLEMS OF SELECTIVE REDUCTION

The published experience of selective reduction is still limited so that a full judgement upon its place in clinical practice must await further information. From the published reports it is clear that selective reduction carries the risk of inducing the abortion of the complete pregnancy in at least a proportion of cases. There is also a theoretical risk of inducing fetal abnormality particularly if the first attempt to induce fetal death is unsuccessful and that pregnancy survives. There has as yet, however, been no published report of an abnormality induced by selective reduction. There is also the potential risk of inducing bleeding or infection associated with any intra-uterine manipulations. In addition, the psychological consequences of selective reduction are unknown and it is possible that grief reactions could be encountered in the parents or even, in the long term, amongst the surviving offspring. These problems are clearly difficult to quantify and answers could only be obtained from careful long term follow up studies.

LEGAL AND ETHICAL PROBLEMS

The proposed procedure of selective reduction presents a large number of potential legal and ethical problems which will be discussed in the next chapter. There is concern that selective reduction might be used as a means to conceal or justify poor clinical practice, allowing doctors to induce high order multiple pregnancies without regard to the consequences. Probably a distinction should be made between deliberately risking the induction of multiple pregnancy with the full intention of using fetal reduction and resorting to fetal reduction only when high order pregnancy occurs inadvertently[6]. A further ethical problem is the arbitrary nature of the decision about which conceptuses will be terminated and which will be saved.

SUMMARY

The incidence of high order multiple pregnancy is increasing as a result of the introduction of the new methods to treat infertility. High order multiple pregnancy carries high risks of mortality or serious long term morbidity in the fetus and of both mortality and morbidity in the mother. The management options of allowing the pregnancy to continue or of terminating the entire pregnancy do not offer fully satisfactory solutions to the problems. Selective reduction of high order multiple pregnancies down to twins in the first trimester has been proposed as an alternative management strategy. Early experience suggests that selective reduction will lead to a comparable number of survivors as anticipated with natural outcome but with substantially reduced morbidity amongst the surviving infants. Although selective reduction raises many ethical and legal problems a strong pragmatic case can be made for its introduction on medical grounds.

REFERENCES

1. Botting B J, Davies I M, Macfarlane A J. Recent trends in the incidence of multiple births and associated mortality. Arch Dis Child 1987; 62: 941–950
2. Evans M I, Fletcher J C, Zador I E. Selective first-trimester termination in octuplet and quadruplet pregnancies: clinical and ethical issues. Obstet Gynaecol 1988; 71, No. 3, 289–296
3. Walker E M, Patel N B. Mortality and morbidity in infants born between 20 and 28 weeks gestation. Br J Obstet Gynaecol 1987; 94: 670–674
4. Levene M I. Grand multiple pregnancies and demand for neonatal intensive care. Lancet 1986; 2: 347–348
5. Hobbins J C. Selective reduction—a perinatal necessity? N Eng J Med 1988; 318: 1062–1063
6. Howie P W. Selective reduction in multiple pregnancy. Br Med J 1988; 664–666
7. Berkowitz R L, Lynch L, Chitkara U et al. Selective reduction of multifetal pregnancies in the first trimester. N Eng J Med 1988; 318: 1043–1047

5. Selective reduction, abortion and the law

Z. Pickup

Throughout its long history, the statutory law of abortion in England and Wales has given rise to problems of interpretation for both doctors and lawyers alike. It is, perhaps, not surprising that many disparate views have been expressed by the two professions concerning the legality or otherwise of clinical abortion practice as determined by their interpretation of statutory language.

As early as 1803[1] on the passing of the first statute to render abortion illegal, it was apparent that contemporary medical practice did not conform with the understanding or intentions of the legislators, as expressed in the Act. The legislators did not provide any statutory defence for these medical men who carried out therapeutic abortion, and also referred to the un-scientific term of 'quickening' which had by then fallen into disrepute within medical circles.

As a consequence, medical men agitated for statutory reform and proposed that all future legislation of a medical nature should be drafted in consultation with medical practitioners to avoid further disparity between the law and medical practice and to prevent the further use of ambiguous terminology in statutes. In 1837 Dr A T Thompson levelled the following criticism at the contemporary legislation: 'A singular instance of the difficulty of rooting out prejudice from the mind ... This distinction with respect to the periods in which criminal abortion is affected demonstrates very strongly the necessity of lawyers and statesmen consulting medical men, prior to framing Acts which involve physiological questions.'[2]

Despite this relevant criticism, quasi-medical statutory language has continued to create confusion and uncertainty for doctors trying to fulfil their duties and obligations within the law and for lawyers attempting to determine the scope of those duties and obligations. Perhaps the most fundamental problem lies in the fact that the substantive law of abortion is contained in a statute passed over a century ago, when, clearly, current developments in medical science and practice could not have been anticipated or envisaged. Consequently, attempts to analyse the legality of contemporary medical practice by reference to a statute which does not address the issues involved in modern technology and which contains ambiguous terminology are frequently self-defeating and problems remain unsolved.

Selective reduction of pregnancy, a recently developed technique, provides a relevant and topical case in point. An examination of the legality, or otherwise, of the technique requires an analysis of the statutory terminology employed in Section 58 of the Offences Against the Person Act 1861 and exposes the ambiguities inherent in that legislation.

The technique involves the killing of one or more fetuses forming part of a multiple pregnancy. Multiple pregnancies have become more common-place through the increasing use in infertility treatment of superovulatory fertility drugs and through the replacement of more than one embryo per menstrual cycle in the uterus of women receiving in vitro fertilisation (IVF) treatment. The procedure may also be used outside the context of fertility treatment, for example, where a woman with a twin pregnancy discovers by amniocentesis or by chorionic villus sampling that one of the twins has a serious handicap. She may wish to terminate the affected twin and allow the other to develop normally[3]. Although there may be a medical or even ethical distinction between selective reduction to reduce numbers and selective feticide, the legal issues will be the same. In both contexts, it may be argued that the technique is therapeutic and preferable to the term-ination of all or both fetuses. For this reason, and despite its moral or ethical debatability, it is probable that the technique will continue to be used and be further refined and developed.

Selective reduction can be employed at less than 10 weeks into the pregnancy when it is simply being used to reduce numbers, or at a later stage when tests have revealed the presence of one or more abnormal fetuses. There are several different techniques which may be used, depending on the stage of gestational development and the preference of the doctor. The fetal sac may be injected with potassium chloride or the fetus may be exsanguinated, aspirated, or destroyed in some other way. Where the fetus is aspirated its expulsion quickly follows the event, whereas with the other methods the fetus will probably remain in situ either mummified or apparently largely or wholly absorbed into the system, and the expulsion which takes place, if at all, occurs at the delivery of the remaining live fetuses[4].

The technique has been carried out in several different hospitals in Britain, but it appears that originally operations did not take place within the provisions of the Abortion Act 1967 since it was considered by medical personnel that there had been no abortion or miscarriage since pregnancy had continued. Indeed, it was reported in 1987 that at least one medical protection organisation had advised its members that the practice does not constitute the offence of abortion at all[5].

It has, however, been pointed out that this view fails to confront the purpose of the abortion law and confuses motive with intent. Since although medical personnel may, and usually will, be acting from the best of motives and in the best interests of their patients, they will nevertheless be intending to terminate the life of one or more fetuses[4].

To determine the legality or otherwise, of the practice, the crucial issue is whether the technique amounts to 'procuring a miscarriage' within the terms of Section 58 of the 1861 Act which stated, *inter alia*:

and, whosoever, with intent to procure the miscarriage of any woman, whether she be or be not with child, shall unlawfully administer to her or cause to be taken by her any poison or other noxious thing, or shall unlawfully use any instrument or other means whatsoever with the like intent, shall be guilty of [an offence], and being convicted thereof shall be liable . . . to [imprisonment] for life . . .

It is necessary to ask what exactly constitutes a miscarriage. Is it constituted by the destruction of the fetus or its expulsion from the mother's body or both?

Confusingly, there are many differing definitions of the terms 'miscarriage' and 'abortion' which are frequently used synonymously. The legal definition of abortion as given by Glanville Williams, is clearer than many medical ones. He states: 'For legal purposes, abortion means feticide: the intentional destruction of the fetus in the womb or any untimely delivery brought about with the intent to cause the death of the fetus.'[6]

This definition concentrates on the killing of the fetus and does not concern itself with the expulsion from the mother's body. It is consistent with the argument, now rendered academic[7], that some methods of contraception, i.e. those which operate after the moment of fertilisation by destroying or preventing the implantation of the blastocyst, offend against the 1861 legislation, since in such cases expulsion of the blastocyst from the mother's body does not necessarily occur.

Medical definitions are considerably more confusing. Most medical dictionaries agree that one meaning of the term 'abortion' is the expulsion of a fetus but they also include alternative definitions. For example, Stedman's Medical Dictionary[8] states one meaning to be 'The arrest of any action or process before its normal completion', and Butterworths Medical Dictionary[9] states: 'Not to reach full development on account of some check'. However, the same medical dictionary further confuses the issue by defining a 'missed abortion' as: 'An abortion in which the embryo or fetus is dead and is retained in the uterine cavity'.

Some techniques of selective reduction could thus fall within this definition of missed abortion. But since the definition refers to a missed abortion as an abortion of a certain type, this argument becomes somewhat circular.

Lay dictionaries are also of little assistance. Websters Seventh New Collegiate Dictionary[10] gives the following definitions: 'Miscarriage' is defined as 'The expulsion of a human fetus before it is viable and especially between the 12th and 24th weeks of gestation'. 'Abortion' is defined as 'The expulsion of a non-viable fetus', and 'spontaneous expulsion of a human fetus during the first twelve weeks of gestation';

thus giving the less common non-synonymous view of the two terms, but nevertheless concentrating on expulsion rather than fetal death. However, the same dictionary later defines 'to abort' as 'to bring forth premature stillborn offspring' and/or 'to become checked in development so as to remain rudimentary or to shrink away'.

This last definition lends credence to the argument that fetal death is the essential factor.

Another argument put forward to support the legality of the technique is that it does not terminate the pregnancy. This view requires consideration of the question: is there one pregnancy per fetus or one pregnancy involving several fetuses? Expressions such as 'multiple pregnancy' can be interpreted to support either viewpoint. Although the predominant medical view would support the argument that pregnancy is the state of being with child regardless of how many or how few fetuses are present. In any event, the words 'termination of pregnancy' do not appear in the 1861 Act which creates the substantive offence, but only in the Abortion Act 1967 which contains the exclusions of liability. Should the matter be litigated the wording of the earlier statute will be of crucial significance.

Ultimately, then, and not surprisingly, arguments revolving around linguistic usage prove self-defeating and inconclusive. They do, however, demonstrate that the ambiguity of definition alone places the legality of the procedure in doubt.

It is possible to argue that such adherence to a black-letter interpretation of the statute may obscure the true purpose underlying the abortion legislation, and that legislative intent should be given due consideration. It is generally accepted that the principal purpose of the legislation is to provide the fetus with a limited degree of protection from termination at will, whilst at the same time making the best possible provision for the mother's continued health and safety. At best, it is a fine balance of interests. To argue that selective reduction falls outside the scope of the Act would leave the fetus forming part of a multiple pregnancy without any form of legal protection. It is neither logical, nor, it is submitted, lawful to create such a distinction. Thus, setting aside any linguistic debate, it is arguable that the practice is flouting the legislative intent of Parliament.

For this reason, it is suggested that the best solution for the medical profession is to assume the practice is unlawful and to rectify this by complying with the provisions of the Abortion Act 1967 whenever such a procedure is carried out. Multiple pregnancy significantly increases the physical risks to the health and life of the pregnant woman, even in the absence of a substantial risk of a seriously handicapped fetus. Morbidity and mortality risks are increased in both mother and babies. Further, the mother's mental health may be prejudiced by the possibility of a multiple birth[11].

Although the technique of selective reduction is so recent a development that the risks attached to it are, as yet, little known it is still highly probable that the risks of continuing the pregnancy will be significantly greater than those involved in selective reduction. There should, therefore, be no real difficulty in practice in complying with the statutory criteria laid down in the 1967 Act to render such procedures lawful. Legally, there may still be problems since such a solution would depend upon the courts interpreting the phrase 'termination of pregnancy' in the 1967 Act to mean one pregnancy per fetus and not one pregnancy per several fetuses, thus not accepting the predominant medical view referred to earlier. If the Abortion Act 1967 does not apply, we are faced with a legislative gap which would mean that the fetus forming part of a multiple pregnancy is unprotected by the law. Doctors may arguably, therefore, be 'procuring a miscarriage' but not 'terminating a pregnancy' thus, falling into a no-man's land between the two statutes. This situation could not have been envisaged by those drafting the legislation in 1967 when it would have been considered impossible to fall foul of one Act without being offered protection by the other.

If on the other hand, the 1967 Act does apply, the implicatons may be far-reaching. If it is accepted that such reduction would be lawful under the 1967 Act because the dangers to both mother and babies of continuing a multiple pregnancy are greater than those involved in reducing it, can it not be argued that the mother may have a right to select which fetuses are terminated and which remain viable? In such circumstances, would it not be lawful to allow her to make a choice based on sex preference? It is submitted that provided the criteria under the 1967 Act are complied with, such sex selection would not be the ground for the abortion, but would merely be a collateral issue, arguably, providing an avenue for the mother to exercise an autonomous choice. In these circumstances such selection would be lawful!

It has been said that 'modern medicine now toys with the concept of the wanted and unwanted'[12] and this may seem particularly true in relation to abortion. A logical corollary may be that if otherwise healthy fetuses are to be terminated because they form part of a multiple pregnancy which is, in itself risky, why should they not, incidentally, be the ones which the mother wants least?

Such a suggestion immediately calls into question the ethics and morality of allowing such a choice. The medical profession may well prefer not to impart to the patient the knowledge they have acquired as to the gender of the fetuses and indeed, it may be deemed preferable to carry out such reduction before fetal gender can be identified to avoid such moral dilemmas. Since the amount of information which a doctor should volunteer to a patient in such circumstances is governed by reference to accepted medical practice[13], such a stance may be legally defensible. But this discussion serves to highlight that in this issue, as in many others, morality and legality may not always coincide.

CONCLUSION

It is clear that problems in assessing the legality or otherwise of new medical techniques in the field of abortion are not going to disappear. Reform or re-examination of existing statute law to take into account modern medical technology and practice is required.

In any such reform it is essential that any quasi-medical terminology intended to be used, should first be considered in consultation with representatives of the medical profession. Only by so doing, could ambiguities of the kind now encountered be avoided. In cases of difficulty, terms could be statutorily defined to assist interpretation.

So far, attempts at reform and re-definition of offences appear to create as many problems as they solve. The Draft Criminal Code[14] which purports only to restate the law, modernises the terminology employed and harmonises the language of the 1861 Act with that used in the Act of 1967. Unfortunately, despite good intentions, the proposed amendments remain ambiguous and would not, for instance, clarify or resolve the issues raised in this paper.

The code removes the word 'miscarriage' from the proposed Clause 70 creating the offences and states that: 'A person who terminates the pregnancy of a woman otherwise than in accordance with the provisions of Section 1 of The Abortion Act 1967 is guilty of an offence.'

This proposal would at least harmonise the language used so that we are faced with one ambiguous phrase rather than two, possibly conflicting, phrases. But 'termination of pregnancy' remains an ambiguity. The expression is not synonymous with 'abortion' and may not require either the death or destruction of the fetus. Medically assisted premature birth such as by Caesarian section could amount to a 'termination of pregnancy'[15].

It appears, then, that the prospects for thorough, specific and non-ambiguous legislation are not encouraging at present. Doctors, in the course of their clinical practice will have to continue to 'second guess' the courts, and sadly, it may be that the sentiments of Dr A T Thompson, first expressed in the nineteenth century[2], will continue to be voiced by his medical successors well into the twenty-first.

REFERENCES

1. Lord Ellenborough's Maiming and Wounding Act. 43 Geo. 3 c.58
2. Dr A T Thompson. Lancet (28 June 1837), p. 626
3. Abortion of a Defective Twin. Discover, August 1981, p. 10
4. D Brahams. Selective Reduction of Pregnancy. L. Soc. Gaz. (1988)
5. The Independent. Tues. 10 March 1987
6. Glanville Williams Textbook of the Criminal Law, 2nd Ed (1983), p. 92
7. See the decision in 1983 of Sir Michael Havers not to prosecute those supplying and administering the post coital pill, and see *Written Answers to Questions*, 10 May 1983. Parl Deb. H.C. Vol. 42, Col. 238, 239

8. Stedmans Medical Dictionary, 24th Ed. 1982
9. Butterworths Medical Dictionary. Butterworth & Co. (1978)
10. Webster's Seventh New Collegiate Dictionary (1970 Ed.)
11. David P T Price. Selective Reduction and Feticide: The Parameters of Abortion. (1988)
    C.L.R. 199, at p. 205
12. Mason & McCall Smith. Law and Medical Ethics, (2nd Ed.) Butterworths (London)
    1987, p. 70
13. Sidaway v Bethlem Royal Hospital Governors and Others [1985] 1 All ER 643 (H.L.)
14. Law Commission; Codification of The Criminal Law: A Report to The Law Commission
    (1985) Law Comm. No. 143
15. Jennifer Temkin. Pre-Natal Injury, Homicide and the Draft Criminal Code [1986]
    C.L.J. 414

6. Discussion for Section 2

K. M. Boyd

By this stage, I suspect, you may be beginning to share my feeling of waking up from a bad dream in the nursery at Bleak House. But let me broaden the discussion from legal issues to moral ones, and four in particular.

First: in his talk, Professor Howie remarks that there would be ethical concern about selective reduction if it were used to conceal or justify poor clinical practice, allowing doctors to induce high order multiple pregnancies without regard for their consequences. That is a question of ethics not of selective reduction, but of clinical practice. It is for practitioners and professional bodies themselves to resolve, by agreeing what is good practice.

Second: among the options other than selective reduction, which Professor Howie mentioned, was allowing the pregnancy to continue. That, he said, had the advantage that it created no ethical or legal problems and spared the parents from the feeling of guilt which might arise from an act of commission. I agree that that may be true of the psychology of the thing, but not of the ethics. To allow the pregnancy to continue, when you know there are likely adverse consequences and you have the means to avoid these, *does* create ethical problems. You cannot avoid the moral responsibility which knowledge imposes on us, by talking selectively in some cases but not in others, about 'letting nature take its course'.

But, third: how is moral responsibility to be exercised? That ethical question, I think, in turn depends upon a metaphysical one, about our philosophy of life, about human nature and our role in nature. It is becoming increasingly apparent from our scientific understanding of reproduction, that in the eary stages of life, a series of processes of natural selection are taking place. Human nature, including science, we could argue, is nature becoming aware of its own workings in us. So our moral responsibility is to co-operate intelligently with the natural processes, and selective reduction may be seen as that, if it is done for good scientific reasons. Against that, it may be argued that selective reduction is just a form of human quality control, which in some sense devalues human nature. But surely part of the value of a pregnancy which comes to term, derives from the vast number of other possible lives which have been sacrificed in order that it may live. Conscientious killing (and the 'conscientious' is crucial) may be compatible with valuing human life.

My final point is to observe that this kind of discussion may lead us into extreme moral individualism which can paralyse action. If it is claimed that every woman has a right to a healthy child, and every conceptus has a right to life, you reach a deadlock. I agree that the choices are incredibly difficult. But if there is some purpose in the universe, part of that purpose may be found in the fact that we have to decide—especially because not acting, when we have the knowledge, *is* acting. It may be by accepting our moral responsibility, including its ambiguity and guilt, that we realise our particular human role in the natural process, and by taking responsibility, discover more clearly what that role is. What are we doing? Are people right to think that this is unnatural? Or, is this a role which nature has imposed upon us, so that we have to work through its difficulties and try to reach some sort of agreement?

Professor Howie, responding to the Chairman's suggestion, returned to Mrs Pickup's question about what was a pregnancy, in relation to one or a group of fetuses. Many doctors, he believed, wished that the lawyers could make up their minds about an agreed definition, so that doctors could know where they stood. Doctors sincerely wanted to help the individual with a problem, and also to work within the law. It was a breach of natural justice that they were, in effect, being told to go ahead and then wait for the courts to decide if they had acted criminally, simply because the lawyers could not make up their minds about definitions. The *Chairman* remarked that the law was made not by lawyers but by society.

Mr David Price (School of Law, Leicester Polytechnic) added that the law was slow on this question because of the lack of consensus in society, and because the lack of criminal prosecutions had not given judges a good chance to express themselves. With reference to Mrs Pickup's remarks, he observed.

1. The offence-creating section of the 1861 Act would undoubtedly be contravened in these cases, because neither the woman's nor the fetus' rights could be protected otherwise. There would be an intrusion but no expulsion from the womb, so that there would be no protection for either party, which was illogical.

2. It seemed ludicrous that the 1967 Act allowed termination of the entire number of fetuses involved but not to select a smaller number. That neither gave effect to the woman's wishes nor protected the remaining fetuses which would otherwise survive.

3. In law, selective feticide was not a separate issue. But if the 1967 Act did not apply, then there was no possibility of carrying out selective feticide either, for the sake of seriously handicapped fetuses.

4. The 1967 Abortion Act focused on the threat to the woman. The fact that other fetuses' health or life might be preserved was not directly addressed.

Professor Steve Smith (Cambridge) suggested that two questions were involved in the discussion: first, how the existing law was interpreted in individual cases; and, second, how medical advances changed how we addressed that law. In both debates this morning they had been hampered by strict legal discussions about what was or was not a miscarriage or an abortion. These questions applied to the past. In the present, a consensus was needed.

Mr S Simmons (Windsor) argued that it was not illogical to immediately reject the idea of selective feticide. One could argue that, if it was permissible to destroy all the fetuses, then you could destroy a few to safeguard the rest. But this was not the way we generally behaved in society. If there were six in a lifeboat, we did not throw overboard or eat three in order that the others should survive. Generally we took our chance and said it would be better all to take the risk than to eat three. Statistically there might even be a case for destroying one normal fetus of twins, but that logic had to take second place to some underlying ethical or behavioural practice.

Dr Boyd commented that the lifeboat example was interesting precisely because some people *had* been thrown overboard or eaten in that eventuality. This illustrated the difficulty of extrapolating from everyday behaviour where resources were adequate, to a situation of drastic scarcity of resources, including those of the womb. In this context how appropriate was it to regard the individual as the ethically prime unit?

Sir Malcolm Macnaughton (Glasgow) suggested that some international comparison might be helpful. The French, for example, were much more pragmatic than the English. If the doctor and patient agreed that a procedure was acceptable, it could be done. The law did not interfere and in France there was very little litigation in this area. The *Chairman* was doubtful about society in this country accepting that approach.

Mr Luke Gormally (Linacre Centre) argued that selective reduction was profoundly repugnant to many people. This was because our concept of justice, which underpinned the criminal law, was based on the equality of all human beings. The equality was a matter simply of our mere humanity. He did not understand Dr Boyd's observation that the value of life derived from the number of lives sacrificed. The value of life derived from the humanity which they all shared. If they were to differentiate between human beings on the basis of acquired or exercisable abilities or characteristics, it would become a matter of choice whom to treat justly or not. Justice in these choices was centrally a matter of intentional action, of the choices that they deliberately effected. Sometimes foreseen consequences had to be lived with. When they could avoid those foreseen consequences in ways which did not involve injustice to others, they might well have a responsibility to do so. But if the only way to avoid foreseeable consequences was by chosen injustice, then unfortunately, they just had to live with the consequences.

Professor David Baird (Edinburgh) wished to emphasise Dr Boyd's point that, as human beings, we did not have the option not to take up the choice. In many parts of the world, increasing misery had been caused by over-population, largely through the improvement of infant survival by medical science. But they had not the choice to withhold treatment for malaria or infectious diseases, in order to allow a smaller proportion of the population to die from malnutrition. The human condition was such that, with the knowledge available for fetal selection, they had to make the decision how to use it, and not just 'let nature take its course'.

Invited to sum up the discussion by the Chairman, *Dr Boyd* remarked that he could best do so in the words of Wittgenstein: 'Of that on which one cannot speak, on that one must be silent.'

Gender selection

7. Prenatal sex selection

M. C. Macnaughton

Many people when asked about sex selection have an immediate reaction that it is not permissible under any circumstances. This gut reaction is not justified when one goes into the matter in greater depth. The technical aspects will be explained so that we know what is involved in these techniques and what is possible at the present time.

With regard to the methods of sex selection, there are 4 possible methods but only 2 are in use at the present time. Amniocentesis is probably the most commonly used method at present. In this method fluid is taken from the uterus around the 16th week of pregnancy and the fetal cells which are present in the fluid are cultured. The geneticists can then examine the chromosomes and determine the sex of the fetus. The disadvantage of this method is that it has to be done relatively late and it is a further 2 weeks before the result is available so that if a termination is required it has to be done at a gestation of 18–20 weeks. This is most unpleasant for all concerned and should be avoided if at all possible.

The second method, which is now available in many centres is Chorion Villus Biopsy (CVB). This has the advantage that it can be done much earlier in pregnancy at around 8–12 weeks. In this method, using ultrasound guidance, a small portion of fetal membranes called the chorion is removed from the uterus without damaging the pregnancy. At this stage of pregnancy these cells are particularly rapidly growing so that they can be quickly grown in the laboratory and examined to determine the sex of the fetus within a few days. This means that the answer regarding the sex of the child can be given very quickly and it is then possible for a termination to be done at a very much earlier stage so that the trauma to the patient is much less. The problem about this method is that the risk of a termination occurring as a result of the procedure is 3% whereas in the case of amniocentesis it is only 0.5%. However, some women are prepared to take the increased risk of CVB to avoid the unpleasantness of having to have a late termination if amniocentesis is used.

The third method mentioned is only at the developmental stage but is quite possible provided that pre-embryo research is allowed to continue. Legislation based on the Warnock Report has now been passed in Parliament[1]. One of the advantages of allowing research to contunue is that this type of technique can be developed whereas it would not be possible without the continuation of research on pre-embryos. In this case eggs are taken from the wife and fertilised by the husband's sperm in the same way as in IVF. When the pre-embryo reaches the 6–8 cell stage, one or two cells are removed by micro manipulation methods. These cells can be sexed by the geneticist. If the embryo is of the wanted sex it is transferred to the wife's uterus as in the IVF procedure and if not it can be allowed to die.

At this stage of development there is no question of termination of pregnancy so that the risks of this to the mother are absent. However, IVF is not a very successful procedure—only 10% of women who have treatment will take home a baby at the end of the day[2]. Therefore, it may be that the woman would not become pregnant at all so this would not be a very satisfactory method unless the success rate can be greatly improved.

The last method involves the separation of X- and Y-bearing sperm[3]. If an egg is fertilised by an X-bearing sperm a female child will result whereas a Y-bearing sperm will result in a male child. Attempts are being made to separate these two different types of sperm so that artificial insemination can be done only with Y-bearing sperm. At the present time the method cannot be guaranteed and much research is still required before this method could be used in practice. This would indeed be a most acceptable method in that it predetermines the sex by facilitating the fertilisation of the ovum with either an X- or Y-bearing sperm.

These then are the methods that are either available or potentially available at present. From a practical point of view, at the present time the first two are the only ones that can be used. There are, of course, old wives' tales such as tying of the left testicle or choosing which side the husband should lie during coitus to ensure a male offspring.

I would now like to mention the reasons for discussing sex selection. In many societies the generation of an offspring carries with it a significance which is disproportionate to the value of the child. The birth of a child of the desired or unwanted sex (usually female) engenders happiness or unhappiness for the parents. Reports of female infanticide in India and China testify to the strength of the underlying emotions evoked. Deeply entrenched traditions, especially in Asian patriarchal societies favour sons to bear the family name, for endowment of inheritance and to provide for social security in old age.

Surveys in the US[4] also showed a strong preference for the first born to be a boy although in a study in Hull in England the majority of newly weds wanted a family of two with one child of each sex[5]. Apart from cultural aspects, and in our pluralistic society in the UK we now have ethnic groups where the traditions just mentioned are strong, there are two more serious reasons for considering sex selection, one of which applies in this country.

The first, which does not really apply in the UK is that in a National Family Planning Programme a family with the desired sex composition would be obtained quickly thereby effectively reducing the total size of the family. The desire for sons or daughters has kept some families from stopping at two. In countries like India and Pakistan with huge population problems this is a real consideration. In some rural areas of China couples are allowed to have two children if the first is a girl.

The second, and perhaps more cogent reason, is to prevent the birth of affected children with sex-linked debilitating diseases like haemophilia or muscular dystrophy. These diseases occur in a child of a particular sex and in a haemophilic family a male child may have a 50:50 chance of having the disease. This second reason is used in the UK at present and comes within the scope of the 1967 Abortion Act. These are the practical aspects of the problem—now what about the ethical aspects as seen from the medical point of view?

In any consideration there are certain ethical principles which have to be observed and these were enunciated in 1979 by an American Government Report from the National Commission for the Protection of Human Subjects—the Belmont Report[6]. Traditionally, Western Ethics has tended to concentrate on ethical relationships among individuals. Other religions and political cultures have given primacy to the collectivity of the group or state as the focal point of ethical concern and have considered the individual owes duties and enjoys rights to protection through membership of the group or nation.

In Western culture, three main ethical principles were laid down in the Belmont Report. The three principles are

1. *Respect for persons*—and there are two parts to this principle. a. Autonomy—this requires that competent people be governed by their own wishes and preferences and that competence be preserved in the case of an adult person, and in adolescence we show on a case to case basis that they possess adequate understanding and a capacity to bear the consequences of autonomous decision-making. b. Protection of the vulnerable—this requires that guardianship be exercised over children, adolescents and impaired adults who are incapable of autonomy.

2. *Beneficence*—this principle goes beyond the negative ethic 'do no harm' by imposing a positive duty to seek good if necessary by initiating action that will advance the welfare of individuals and communities.

3. *Justice*—this principle is directed to the achievement of fairness in dealings among peoples, for instance by seeking to ensure that the intended beneficence of a development will bear its risks and pay its costs appropriately and that one group of people will not be sacrificed for the benefit of another.

Some of these ethical principles will appear to be violated if one subscribes to the view that an embryo or fetus is entitled to the same rights and protection as an adult but this is by no means a universal view. A year ago at its meeting in Munster, the Standing Committee on Ethical Aspects of Human Reproduction of the International Federation of Gynaecology and

Obstetrics (FIGO) discussed this matter and submitted a statement to the Executive Board. This document is important in the context of this discussion. As you might expect the first statement simply says that with regard to sex selection the committee could not reach an agreement. This is not surprising as the committee comprises members from 14 different countries and many different cultures.

The first point is that the ethical principle of protection of the vulnerable, i.e. the pre-embryo or fetus, and the ethical principle of justice are violated by sex selection abortion and that no fetus should be sacrificed because of its sex alone. Most members of the committee accepted this but members from countries like India had doubts about this statement and from what has been said before this is understandable.

The next point was to do with Women's Rights and says that the ethical principles of autonomy of the woman is violated by complete prohibition of sex selection abortion. This really means that the woman has a right to say what should happen to her and in some countries with particular cultures they would object to prohibition on these grounds.

The next point is very pertinent to the present time and says that techniques for sex selection, although not yet perfect, will probably be developed in the near future. This refers to the separation of the X- and Y-bearing sperm and to the IVF techniques already mentioned. The addendum that research should be allowed to proceed because of its potential benefits is very important to stress at this time when there are doubts as to whether this will be allowed to continue or not.

The strong medical reason for sex selection that many of us in this country now accept and which is widely practised as part of antenatal care is the use of sex selection to avoid sex-linked genetic disorders. This is justified on medical grounds.

The next point is concerned with social grounds for sex selection. Sex selection can be justified on social grounds in certain cases for the objective of allowing children of the two sexes to enjoy the loving care of parents. For this social indication to be justified it must not conflict with other society values where it is practised.

This is important in this country because we have here now many people with a traditional culture which would justify sex selection on social grounds. However, in the UK—a Western culture society—it would conflict with Western society values and therefore would be unacceptable. Having said that, however, there can be a dilemma for us in this context. If someone living in the UK, but coming from a society with different cultural traditions, where a son is important for reasons already mentioned seems unable to have one and has a number of girls, if she becomes pregnant the pressures of her culture and the anxiety generated by the thought that she may be carrying a child of the 'wrong' sex could lead to a state of psychiatric disturbance where, in order to prevent her from damaging herself by attempting abortion or even suicide, it was in her best interests to know the sex of the child and to allow termination if it were of the 'wrong' sex. In such an extreme case, sex selection abortion could be justified under the present Act. This would be an extreme rarity but is a possibility.

Lastly, prenatal sex selection should never be used as a tool for sex discrimination against either sex, especially female.

It will be seen that there could appear to be some conflict between some of the points and they are put forward in a way which shows that compromise at an international level has to be arrived at.

Finally, one can conclude that sex selection procedures for unwanted sex are unacceptable in Western cultures unless for the prevention of inherited disease but when one looks at the problem on a World basis other factors have to be taken into account.

REFERENCES

1. Report of the Committee of Inquiry into Human Fertilization and Embryology (1984)—Chairman Dame Mary Warnock—London: HM Stationery Office
2. Fourth Report of the Voluntary Licensing Authority for Human in vitro Fertilization and Embryology, 1989, p. 19, The Voluntary Licensing Authority (London)
3. Chia C M and Ratnam S S. Sex preselection—how close to reality? Singapore Journal of Obstetrics and Gynaecology, 1983, 14: 111–117
4. Westoff C F and Rindfuss R. Sex preselection in the United States: some implications. Science 1974, 184: 633–636
5. Peel J. The Hull family survey. Journal of Biosocial Science 1970, 2: 45–70
6. National Commission for the Protection of Human Subjects of Biomedical and Behavioral Research (1979). Ethical Principles and Guidelines for the Protection of Human Subjects of Research, Washington: US Government Printing Office

8. Legal and ethical dilemmas of fetal sex identification and gender selection

D. Morgan

Gender denotes legal, social and economic distinctions that follow from biological difference. Sex denotes the biological classification of human beings into two broad categories[1].

... it would be possible, using in vitro fertilisation, to allow a number of eggs to develop to a stage at which the sex of each organism could be determined. Those of the unwanted sex could be jettisoned, and one of the desired sex implanted. Rather as with a litter of kittens, one could keep the boys and throw the girls away, but long before birth. ... Obviously, the use of such a procedure in human beings raises in acute form questions of the sanctity of life. In the broad human sense, nothing has been lost: a person who wished to procreate has done so. In a narrow sense, thousands, even millions of potential organisms have been sacrificed[2].

The economic dilemma of modern medicine arises partly from the fact that many medical advances improve the survival of people with chronic disabilities, and so lead to increasing service needs. Largely because of this, in the absence of prevention, the cost of treating patients with inherited diseases (such as cystic fibrosis, sickle cell disease, phenylketonuria, haemophilia, thalassemia and Huntington's chorea) will double in the next 20–30 years. Unlike many other branches of medicine, medical genetics has a built in means through genetic counselling and prenatal diagnosis for limiting its own expansion[3].

INTRODUCTION

What I am primarily concerned with in this essay are issues of *gender*, in which the sex of the embryo or fetus is 'identification evidence' on the basis of which other decisions are taken. To be sure, the balance between the emphasis given to sex and that to gender is not a constant, fixed one. When I am discussing the use of diagnostic and screening procedures for the identification of X-linked inherited disease, I am primarily concerned with the question of the sex of the fetus. But even in this case, I contend that the conclusions which are drawn are based upon a series of assumptions or beliefs which are intimately connected with economic and social, as well as moral and legal values and judgments. When I move to discuss fetal sex identification and abortion, I am primarily and explicitly concerned with questions of gender.

This paper proceeds in two parts. In Part I, I review various techniques which may be used to identify the sex of a fetus or embryo. Thereafter, I move to examine the question of Prenatal Screening, Prenatal Diagnosis and Genetic Information. Here, I look briefly at the incidences of and screening for congenital malformation, chromosomal abnormality and inherited disease. There follows the first of two evaluative sections in the paper. Here I attempt to identify some of the ethical and legal concerns to which Part I gives rise and review two groups of response. First, that of the United Kingdom's White Paper on Human Infertility Services and the succeeding legislation. Secondly, the Council of Europe's Ad Hoc Committee of Experts in the Biomedical Sciences (CABHI), Draft Recommendation on Prenatal Genetic Screening, Prenatal Genetic Diagnosis and Associated Genetic Counselling. This concluding section in Part I is called 'The search for the perfect baby?'.

Part II of the paper examines fetal sex identification for the purposes of abortion on the grounds of the fetus's gender. I examine the impressionistic data for the prevalence of gender selection, the wider context for son preference, the ambit of the Abortion Act 1967, and finally the reproductive ethics implicated by this use of modern technology. This closing section is entitled 'The search for the perfect society?'.

A preliminary point needs here to be addressed. Pre-natal diagnosis and genetic screening, fetal gender identification and questions of random reduction of multiple pregnancies[4] raise a range of legal and ethical questions. In this paper, I am going to concentrate on only some of the legal issues, notably, fetal sex identification and abortion, counselling, confidence and consent, and only a selective range of the ethical dilemmas. It may be appropriate, however, to identify part of the broader range of questions which a full consideration of this topic would demand. For example, with diagnosis and screening, it needs to be recognised that these have wider ethical and legal implications than those flowing simply from diagnosis and screening based on sex. Other important consequences flow for chromosomal and multi-factorial diseases. In addition, each of these areas raise questions, sometimes different questions, of counselling and negligence, counselling and confidentiality, and actions based upon a claim for wrongful life.

In a paper of this compass I cannot, indeed I do not, hope to deal with all such issues. It is important, however, that they are identified for discussion elsewhere. Similarly, with the question of random reduction, there are questions such as whether this constitutes an abortion, whether numbers can in themselves constitute a ground for abortion under the Abortion Act 1967, and so on. Fortunately, these matters are expertly dealt with elsewhere[5].

Finally, there are a group of ethical questions associated with diagnosis and screening, which might be roughly reduced to questions about societal attitudes to handicap and disability more generally. A fuller argument of these than that presented here would suggest that questions of diagnosis and screening can and indeed should be properly separated from attitudes towards handicap and disability, or towards people with different learning and other social abilities. It is sometimes suggested that attitudes towards testing, screening and even appropriate treatment regimes for severely-handicapped neonates is somehow *necessarily* connected with the way in which we view, provide for or abuse disabled or differently capable people in modern Western society. In fact, it would be a fool who suggested that such a paradise already existed, and probably an able-bodied and able-minded fool at that. But this need not, indeed should not shield us from the fact that there can be attitudes towards handicap which are not based on discrimination but on compassion, that technology and screening can bring understanding as well as ignorance, hope as well as despair. To achieve the necessary balance between the benefits which technology and knowledge can bring and the reinforcement of attitudes of repugnance and discrimination is not an easy task. But it confuses rather than clarifies the issue to claim that screening, diagnosis and, say, abortion, necessarily reinforce negative attitudes. They may do, and any tendencies towards that should be resisted. Without these understandings, we assume awesome power without responsibility. And, unless we are to accept a totalitarianism of the abled, we should want to guard against and reject this.

PART I

HOW CAN SEX BE DETERMINED?

Recently, attempts to realise techniques of sperm selection have been practised; a team at Keio University in Japan is reported as having used a centrifugal system to isolate the differential densities of X and Y chromosomes carried in sperm in order to produce an X chromosome rich fraction. This sperm was then used to artificially inseminate six women who specifically wanted to bear a female child[6].

A second method involves the sexing of embryos prior to, or soon after implantation. This can be done by taking a small piece of tissue from the developing embryo or by dividing the eight-cell stage embryo into two and, using DNA probes to recognise part of the Y chromosome, examining one half while the other is freeze-stored pending the outcome of the DNA examination. A more recent variation on these cumbersome DNA procedures is PCR—Polymerase Chain Reaction. This involves amplifying specific segments of the DNA code exponentially, without the necessity of cloning the DNA into a vector, such as a virus or bacteria, which was previously done. Two small pieces of DNA—primers—are stuck to and flank the DNA region to be amplified. These primers are used to synthesise the copy. Between 20 and 40 cycles of amplification are performed, with the DNA *doubling* at each cycle. One reported application[7] of this technique has produced fetal sexing for X-linked conditions. This was achieved from a single cell from a human embryo at the 6–10 cell cleavage (about 3 days after in vitro fertilisation). The cell was broken open in a test tube and the DNA released. A section was then taken on the Y chromosome and amplified up using PCR. This produced sufficient DNA to observe it with conventional analytical techniques. One result of this sort of application is that it becomes possible to sex a *single cell*, because the Y specific fragment will give no signal from a female cell, whereas there will be one from a male cell. The advantages of PCR are that it does not interfere with the development of the embryo; intervention can be performed at a very early stage of development, with the prospect of speedy results of the DNA analysis (for carriers of cystic fibrosis genes results have been tendered in 10 hours). PCR has also been applied to individual sperm, but the presence of dust particles (usually human skin) have been shown to produce a lot of false negative and positive results. 'Using this method, population screening will be possible using single hairs, or cells from mouth washings, thus saving the time and expense of taking blood samples.'[8] These techniques could also be used for pre-implantation diagnosis of the early ovum or blastocyst in vitro before return to a woman's uterus. The limitations presently are that little is known about the resilience of the pre-embryo under such manipulation. These possibilities underpin the calls for research on such embryos to continue uninterrupted, despite the spectre of legislation which would render such research unlawful[9].

Thirdly, there is a group of diagnostic procedures which may involve determining fetal sex during pregnancy, or which may be used solely for diagnostic purposes. Five such techniques can be identified here:

1. Amniocentesis; this involves drawing off amniotic fluid from the amniotic sac in which the developing fetus is harboured and culturing the fetal cells so obtained to distinguish between the XX (female) and XY (male) cells so obtained. Despite claims made by some clinics, notably in Northern India, it is not possible to produce a result from amniocentesis quickly. Culturing the cells takes several weeks and, as amniocentesis can only be performed after the 16th week of pregnancy, any resulting decision in relation to abortion is well into the 20th week of the pregnancy.

2. Chorionic villus sampling, CVS, demands the biopsy of a few cells from the fingers of tissue (the villi) which grow from the chorion (the membrane, derived from the early embryo surrounding the fetus) into the wall of the uterus. Such sampling can be done after six to eight weeks of pregnancy, and the results of the DNA analysis can be made available within 48 hours, although the time taken for diagnosis can range from three days to three weeks[10].

3. Fluorescence-activated cell sorting, FACS, involves the identification of fetal blood cells that have crossed the placenta into the mother's blood or the use of blood samples taken directly from the fetus. It can be performed safely only after the 17th week of pregnancy. The technique now

practised of ultrasound guided transabdominal needle puncture of the fetal cord insertion also allows fetal skin and liver biopsies, selective feticide of one discordant twin and intrauterine transfusions[11].

4. Ultrasound scanning can be used in order to determine the sex of the fetus, but only after the development of external genitalia, during the third trimester of pregnancy, and even then, identification of the relevant organ is difficult, even to a trained operator. Whereas the other methods identified can be used with relatively high success rates, the use of ultrasonography for sex identification purposes is not particularly reliable.

5. DNA methods of examination and diagnosis have been introduced above. These are increasing greatly the range and accuracy of prenatal and carrier diagnosis for inherited disease. The chromosomal locations of defective genes that cause about 600 single gene disorders have now been identified[12].

WHAT MIGHT SELECTION BE USED FOR?

There are three potential reasons for the use of sex selection; 1. the negative eugenic elimination of sex-linked disease; 2. the establishment of a unisex society or community; 3. a preference for sons. In this paper, I want primarily to concentrate on the first and the third of these as raising linked issues. The second clearly is related, but raises somewhat different concerns.

PRENATAL SCREENING, PRENATAL DIAGNOSIS AND GENETIC INFORMATION

Prenatal screening can be used to identify from among a population of apparently healthy individuals those whose risk of a specific genetic disorder that may affect the fetus is sufficiently high so as to justify a subsequent diagnostic test or procedure. Prenatal diagnosis is used to confirm or reject whether a specific genetic abnormality which might affect the fetus is present in an individual pregnant woman at high risk.

One to two per cent of all newborns have a major congenital or genetically determined disorder. Few can be treated satisfactorily; management if possible is burdensome, expensive and often thought to be unsatisfactory. Two to three per cent of couples are at high and recurrent risk of having children with an inherited disorder. These include: dominant disorders (where disease occurs even if only one copy of the two copies of each gene inherited by an individual is defective), such as Huntington's chorea, neurofibromatosis, multiple polyposis coli or adult polycystic kidney disease; X-linked disorders, which are determined by genes located on the X chromosome, hence sex-linked traits, such as fragile mental retardation, Duchenne muscular dystrophy and Haemophilia A; and finally recessive disorders, (where disease occurs only if both copies of an inherited gene are affected), such as cystic fibrosis and phenylketonuria, and in certain ethnic groups, thalassemia, sickle cell disease and Tay-Sachs disease. Carriers of many of these diseases may increasingly be detected by biochemical or DNA methods. According to the Royal College of Physicians, the goal of genetic and prenatal diagnostic provision must be 'to help these couples make an informed choice, one which they feel is best for themselves and their families[13].

The diagnosis of a dominant disorder in one individual implies a risk for all first degree relatives of carrying the same pathological gene and of developing the same disease and transmitting it to their offspring. The vast majority of abnormal genes carried in human populations are recessive and most people carry at least one such potentially lethal gene[14].

Screening for congenital malformations

Congenital malformations may be 'screened for' in one of three ways; infectious causes, maternal serum alphafetoprotein estimation or ultrasound scanning. The main source of infectious congenital malformation is the rubella virus. Although only about 20% of exposed fetuses will be affected, evidence of maternal exposure leads often to therapeutic abortion. Presently, definitive prenatal diagnosis is possible only at about 22 weeks' gestation. Testing for virus DNA in CVS procedures may make the detection of fetal rubella infection possible in the first trimester in the future.

Alphafetoprotein (AFP) is a fetal plasma protein. When a malformation such as neural tube defect occurs, it allows some of the AFP to leak into the amniotic fluid and some into the maternal circulation. A raised maternal serum AFP should lead to level 3 (expert) ultrasound scanning[15].

Screening for chromosomal anomalies

The diagnostic method most used here is amniocentesis, or CVS followed by karyotyping (chromosomal analysis). Because there are obstetric risks and karyotyping is a skilled and labour-intensive procedure, pre-natal testing for fetal chromosomal anomalies is usually offered only to women at more than 0.5–1.0% risk of bearing a child with Down's Syndrome. Most Down's Syndrome children are now born to young mothers[16]. The developmental retardation of Down's Syndrome fetuses is often reflected in below-average maternal serum AFP. With this routine screen, integrated with maternal age, pregnant women at more than 0.5% risk are already identified. This is thought to give a good guide to about a third of all women with a Down's Syndrome fetus. A definitive diagnosis could then be offered with amniocentesis. This proportion could be raised to 50% of Down's Syndrome fetuses through a combination of other indicators.

Screening for inherited diseases

The feasibility of carrier detection is an important limiting factor here. It is presently possible to detect before pregnancy only for relatives of patients with a limited number of dominant or X-linked disorders, and for recessively inherited haemoglobin disorders and Tay-Sachs disease. The possibilities using developing DNA methods are however immense. The next decade will likely bring specially-constructed genetic probes to detect carriers and provide prenatal diagnosis for the commonest inherited diseases. In addition, PCR will make this work much cheaper, and potentially, far less invasive.

Cystic fibrosis is the most common recessively-inherited disease in the UK. Pre-natal diagnosis is possible with an assay of amniotic fluid at 19 weeks' gestation or DNA analysis in the first trimester, and PCR. Although there is an increasing demand for the service, it has only a small effect on the birth rate of affected children because no carrier testing yet exists and prenatal diagnosis can only be offered to couples retrospectively, i.e. after the birth of a first affected child. Prospective carrier diagnosis would require the prior testing of the whole population before they have children. As the RCP Report expresses it: 'Important advances are now pending for cystic fibrosis, the gene for which is carried by about 5% of the UK population. When a DNA-based method for carrier screening becomes available, the high incidence of carriers *implies that screening should be offered to all people prior to reproduction*'[17]. This raises issues of compulsion, compellability and confidentiality, all major sources of ethical disquiet. I shall return to consider these points later.

The use of diagnosis for the elimination of such sex-linked diseases as haemophilia (carried on the X chromosome) or Duchenne Muscular Dystrophy, and of sex determination techniques in the identification of individuals at risk of passing on dominant disorders, or chromosome disorders, such as Down's Syndrome, Edward's Syndrome, could hardly be described as uncontested. For many people, however, they probably represent one of the acceptable faces of genetics.

THE SEARCH FOR THE PERFECT BABY?

While it may be true that the development of these techniques has already brought the relief of much pain and suffering to the lives of identifiable human subjects, they nonetheless raise issues of acute ethical difficulty. They raise, in Jonathan Glover's memorable phrase, the question 'What sort of people should there be?' What characteristics should those who are yet to be born possess? We may find a large degree of agreement about the answers given to some parts of that question; areas of divergence to others. We have to find ways of mediating these different responses, of approaching our own responses defensibly, and of drawing boundary lines which, while having all the appearances of arbitrariness, can be defended, if not logically, then at least consistently.

The only effective way of putting to practical use the findings of many of these diagnostic techniques is to abort an identifiable fetus. For some opponents of abortion, this fact is sufficient in itself to render the process morally indefensible. Indeed, there is evidence which suggests that some women are put under pressure by their attendant physicians to consider abortion as a prerequisite of any testing.

In a mistaken attempt to justify the obstetric risk and expense involved in pre-natal testing, women are often asked for an undertaking to terminate the pregnancy should the fetus prove to be affected. Insensitive handling during termination of pregnancy is common. If pregnancy is to be terminated, the need for support and for subsequent contact is the same as that required for high risk conditions[18].

As the RCP Report comments, it is perhaps not surprising that there is some public anxiety about the medical application of genetic knowledge[19]. Now, while the legality of such diagnostic procedures, and indeed the subsequent abortion of an affected fetus is not thought to be at doubt under United Kingdom law, it is the question of ethics which arises most acutely.

However, let me very briefly recall the legal position. It is what may be called 'the unexamined ground' of abortion law[20]. It is as well to set out in full the operative provisions of the Abortion Act 1967 here, because reference will be made to it throughout the remainder of the paper. Section 1 of that Act provides:

Subject to the provisions of this section, a person shall not be guilty of an offence under the law relating to abortion when a pregnancy is terminated by a registered medical practitioner if two medical practitioners are of the opinion, formed in good faith:
(a) that the continuance of the pregnancy would involve risk to the life of the pregnant woman, or of injury to the physical or mental health of the pregnant woman or any existing children of her family, greater than if the pregnancy were terminated; or
(b) that there is a substantial risk that if the child were born it would suffer from such physical or mental abnormalities as to be seriously handicapped.

Notice, importantly, that the Act does not say that a fetus may be aborted if it is carrying undesirable genes. Section 1(1)(b) requires that the physician decide that there is a 'substantial' risk that the physical or mental abnormalities are such that the child if born would be 'seriously' handicapped. Of course, termination on the grounds of fetal abnormality may additionally be justified under s1(1)(a), that the woman is so worried about continuing the pregnancy that it deleteriously affects her mental or physical health, but that is not the point with which I am immediately concerned. I am interested to know what sufficiency is required for a termination under s1(1)(b) alone.

The question arises, what standard is to be applied when deciding on the degree of 'serious handicap'. One immediate analogy which could be drawn upon is provided by the neonate. In two recent cases, the Court of Appeal has had to consider in what, if any, circumstances a severely handicapped infant might be allowed to die. In *Re C*[21] a baby born with an unusually severe form of hydrocephalus and with a poorly-formed brain structure was allowed to die. She was physically handicapped, including generalised spastic cerebral palsy of all limbs, probable blindness and deafness and an inability to absorb food. In the first judgment of its kind, the High Court acknowledged *and condoned* the paediatric practice of managing some neonates towards their death rather than striving with heroic interventions to save or treat at all costs. The review by the Court of Appeal has now produced the position that the appropriate criteria against which a non-treatment decision may be taken is a legal question for determination by the courts, the actual taking of that decision is one for the parents and the medical team dealing with a particular case.

Re C fleshed out the skeletal approach which the Court of Appeal had said should be brought to these cases in its earlier judgment in *Re B*[22]. There, the Court had established that these cases could only proceed under a 'best interests' (in that case of the ward) test and secondly, that only in a case where the prognosis established that the child's future life was going to be 'demonstrably . . . so awful' and where there was no lingering doubt that a non-treatment order would be appropriate. This would include cases of severe proved damage where the future was so uncertain that the court would be driven to conclude that non-treatment was appropriate. Such cases would not, however, arise, where the prognosis or information about the damage was 'still so imponderable' that it would be wrong for the baby to be allowed to die.

In *Re C*, Mr Justice Ward at first instance, in a part of his judgment which does not appear to have been questioned by the Court of Appeal, identified two criteria, relational and physiological, which will ensure that non-treatment orders will be narrowly drawn[23]. He said that the ward had suffered 'severe and irreparable damage' and that she was 'permanently unable to interact mentally, socially and physically'. Tying these standards to the extensively-rehearsed facts of the case gives an indication of the sort of case in which the courts are going to hold non-treatment to be appropriate and acceptable *in the child's own best interests*.

There are two points here which need clarification. First, in drawing this analogy between the 'treat to die' cases and the fetal ground of s.1(1)(b), I am not suggesting that all fetuses necessarily demand the same protection as all children and adults[24]. Although *Re B* and *Re C* were both concerned with babies in their early months, nothing in those decisions straight-forwardly suggests that they are applicable only to newborns[25]. However, sound arguments could be adduced to support a position which placed fetuses and neonates in a band of protection which differed from that accorded to older children and adults.

Secondly, in addition to the unarticulated limits of these cases is the court's failure to acknowledge that neonates are regularly 'not-treated' in neonatal units on broader criteria than those approved and applied in *Re B* and *Re C*[26]. If it is accepted that neonates may attract different protection from that afforded to older children and adults, it may be argued (it does not follow, of course) that there should be some consistency between the interpretation given to s.1(1)(b), paediatric practices and the judicial criteria for non-treatment.

The point of this excursus is simple, but important. In considering what serious handicaps qualify under section 1(1)(b), it is at least arguable that it covers *only* those where it can be shown that the child's life will be so demonstrably awful that it will be in the *child's interests for it to be aborted while a fetus*. This would follow if one accorded to the fetus a status similar to or comparable with the neonate, or the severely-handicapped neonate. If those states are not to be equated, grounds for differentiation need to be adduced. Of course, if we eschew the notion of a metaphysical frontier, there is the possibility that, say abortion and non-treatment should be treated differently, perhaps because the reasons supporting them are of different weight, in just the same way that, say, abortion and embryo research may be treated differently[27].

Glanville Williams has suggested that the fetal ground for abortion relates to the welfare of the parents, whose lives may be 'blighted by having to rear a grossly defective child', and 'perhaps secondly by consideration for the public purse'[28]. His supporting reasoning is not immune from questioning. Morally, as Williams points out, this seems to involve the commitment that the fetus is not the same as a child, for the killing of children because of their handicap is not permitted. But, as I have shown, such killing is indeed condoned, *where it can be shown to be in their own best interests*. This qualification is not observed by Williams.

It is clear from *Re B* and *Re C* that 'treating for dying' is justified as being in the child's best interests. That is not what Williams has suggested is contemplated under the Abortion Act. He has argued that the welfare to be considered is that of the parents. If this is correct, and that is not conceded, my argument is this. If the ground on which a child can be relieved of the burden of life in its own interests is narrowly drawn, as it is under *Re C* and *Re B*, it is arguable that the necessary conditions to be satisfied for relieving *others* under the 'fetal abnormality' grounds of the Abortion Act should be comparable. It is arguable that they ought, at the very least, to be no more widely drawn; arguably that they should be drawn in the same place, and even arguably that they should be drawn more narrowly than criteria which are to be applied in deciding on treatment for the *child's own interests*.

However, many of those who argue that handicapped neonates can properly be allowed to die (and as I argue above, the same argument could apply *a fortiori* to fetuses) do so on grounds which *combine* the interests of the neonate and her family. If this were not so, and the only interests which fell to be considered were those of the fetus or neonate, it might be difficult to resist an argument for the compellability of an abortion *against a pregnant woman's wishes*, which most people would find objectionable. This is discussed below. Furthermore, Williams' contention that a relatively-low risk of a relatively-severe handicap would justify termination under s.1(1)(b)[29] cannot be sustained. In all cases the ground is clear, it has to be shown not merely that there is a chance or even a risk of the fetus developing into a child which would suffer from such physical or mental abnormalities as to be seriously handicapped, but that there is a *substantial* risk, (i.e. much greater than 50% risk), that this will be the case.

It follows from this that the *lawfulness* of a termination on the grounds of, say carrying an X-linked disease is not straightforward, and cannot be justified on section 1(1)(b) grounds *alone* merely on the basis of its existence. This legal question is, of course, itself independent from the ethical dilemmas to which genetic screening and prenatal diagnosis give rise. Two types of ethical dilemma might be identified; I will call them the internal ethical dilemma and the external ethical dilemma.

The internal ethical dilemma

One 'internal' dilemma I take to be generated by such practices as that which the RCP Report rebuked. It is axiomatic that it cannot be acceptable, for example, that women should be harried towards decisions on the grounds of cost, convenience or conscience of the doctor. The RCP Report recognises this when its review of ethical aspects of the practices considered states that women must have the right to refuse testing[30], that couples should never be pressed to terminate an affected pregnancy and that a doctor opposed to abortion may not deprive a pregnant woman of access to pre-natal diagnosis. It is obligatory for a doctor who in conscience opposes abortion to refer a woman to another doctor who will make the necessary facilities available[31].

A similar range of sentiments informs the review produced by the Ad Hoc Committee of Experts in the Biomedical Sciences (CABHI) of the Council of Europe in April 1989[32]. This has recommended the introduction into each contracting state of legislation which will ensure the regulation of screening and diagnostic tests according to a number of established principles. Of the 13 principles which emerge from their discussions, the following seem of particular ethical importance in this 'internal' sense.

1. Prior counselling should be a *sine qua non* of any screening or diagnosis (Principle 1). Counselling should aim to transcend the provision of the mere medical and scientific terms and to be adapted to the level of knowledge and psychological situation of the couple.

2. Prenatal screening and diagnosis tests should be aimed only at detecting a serious risk to [the] health of the child (Principle 2). It does not

specify whether this is physical or mental health, but it does state that tests should be directed particularly to those conditions for which treatment can be given during pregnancy or immediately after birth. They should not be employed to detect abnormalities which are of minor significance and should never be used to verify characteristics which have nothing to do with congenital abnormalities. They should not, for example, be used to establish the sex of the future child other than for sex-linked diseases. (I deal with this point in Part II.) Unexpected findings discovered during a prenatal screening or diagnosis should usually be communicated to the woman/couple who must then be counselled about the results.

3. Counselling must be non directive (Principle 4). The counsellor should never attempt to impose her or his own religious, philosophical or other convictions on the pregnant woman/couple. The counsellor should obtain no financial benefit from a particular outcome of the counselling.

4. Prenatal genetic screening and diagnosis may only take place with the free and informed consent of the woman (Principle 6). It is important to stress the ambit of this principle, because it stands in contrast to Principle 5 which states that the participation of both partners in the counselling sessions should be encouraged. This raises squarely the question of who is involved in the genetic screening, and the differential responsibilities which are implicated. I think that this distinction between counselling and consent is an important one. The confusion, indeed conflation of the interests of the individual partners with and into the interests of the couple is unfortunate and devoid of any legal significance. It is important that consents be obtained from each partner, but only to those procedures which affect them as individuals, and not as some fictional entity.

The CABHI states the principle underlying this argument clearly and concisely.

The medical ethics of all states require that any medical act must be carried out with the free and informed consent of the person who is expected to undergo it. As the tests of prenatal screening or diagnosis are to be made on the pregnant woman, she is the only person who can give or refuse consent to such tests. . . . The question arises, when she agrees, whether the additional consent of the future father will also be required. The majority of experts were against requiring such additional consent . . . but the CABHI . . . preferred to leave this matter to national law.

5. Consent should not be constrained by requirements of national law or administrative practice (Principle 8). Entitlements, e.g. to medical insurance or social allowances should not be made dependent on having undergone tests or diagnoses. Interesting here is the CABHI response to the requirement of the Greek Orthodox Church in Cyprus. Before celebrating a marriage between Greek Cypriots, the Church requires a certificate proving that a genetic screening test for thalassaemia has taken place. CABHI responded by observing that the test is not demanded by the state authority, but by the precepts of an independent authority and is

justified when entire nations or regions are threatened by genetic illness. The results of the test are not revealed to the church authorities. It is of further interest to note that 98% of screened couples who discover they are both carriers nonetheless follow through with their intention to marry[33].

6. The generation, processing, storage and release of genetic information should be closely controlled (Principles 11 and 12). The only justification for collection and storage of genetic information is for medical use. Long-term conservation of genetic data is justified because it may concern several generations, or a disease may not appear until late in life. Such storage gives rise to security implications, access implications, (whether by the data subject direct or only through a physician), and the collection and storage of genetic information on genetic relatives unknown to those persons. CABHI takes the views that subject to national variations, it should not be mandatory to advise individually these relatives of the existence of relevant stored data.

This gives rise to some particular difficulties. For example, it is a difficult question whether once the information about genetic make-up is available, there is a moral or legal duty to use that information, and to whom it should be circulated[34]. Similarly, once genetic screening techniques are available, there may arise liability in negligence on behalf of either a counsellor or doctor for either a failure to alert a patient to this, or who carries out a screening procedure in such a negligent fashion that it fails to disclose the presence of an affected fetus. I do not have the space here for an extended discussion of these issues, but two points are worthy of note.

First, in the Californian case of *Tarasoff* v *Regents of the University of California*[35], the courts imposed liability on a psychiatrist who failed to warn a person of his client's stated intent, later effected, to murder her. The victim's family recovered damages. Subsequent cases have extended this principle to impose liability on psychiatrists who fail to *detect and warn* of a danger. This could form the basis of an argument of a similar common law duty to warn of impending genetic risk, even to the extent of over-riding the doctor or counsellor's duty of confidentiality to her or his immediate patients[36].

The difficulty with such arguments is that British courts and legislature have set themselves against so-called wrongful life suits brought by people whose claim is for damages to compensate them for having been born following failure of prenatal diagnostic testing[37]. The courts in the United States and the United Kingdom have allowed recovery for wrongful birth actions. Here, the parents' claim is based on the same facts but seeking to recover for the costs of the upbringing of the child who had they been correctly advised would have been aborted[38].

Interestingly, the White Paper *Human Fertilisation and Embryology: A Framework for Legislation* does not address the questions of prenatal screening and diagnosis directly. It describes the genetic manipulation of the embryo to allow the creation of human beings with certain pre-determined characteristics as one which 'society would clearly regard as ethically unacceptable'[39] and the Human Fertilisation and Embryology Bill recently published at the time of writing proposes that legislation would prohibit this[40]. Beyond that, however, the concerns of the White Paper and the resulting legislation are concerned more with questions related to assisted conception and research than with the central matters of this essay. It may be that the framework established within that specific context of assisted reproduction will form the blueprint for legislative consideration of genetic disease screening more generally. For the moment, however, the transmission of hereditary disease, sex selection whether of the embryo before fertilisation occurs or of an existing embryo or fetus, and clinical and social reasons for sex or gender identification are not the subject of Parliamentary scrutiny[41].

A third type of internal question addresses the *scope* of research on genetic disorders. Here, controversy focuses on disorders which may also have an environmental impact, such as coronary heart disease, diabetes, some malignancies, manic depressive disorders and schizophrenia. The arguments concern whether these are environmentally or socially caused or created and that genetic mapping has nothing to offer here whatsoever and that, if there are environmental causes or contributory causes, these should be examined or avoided before prenatal diagnosis is introduced. There is also what the RCP report calls the 'borderline situation', such as the carrier state for familial hypercholesterolaemia or the emphysema-producing form of alpha 1 antitrypsin deficiency or a strong disposition to diabetes, where the 'possibilities for accurate prediction of risk for multifactorial diseases will increase'. They conclude that 'ultimately the attitudes, experience, and wishes of parents and society at large will determine their application for prenatal diagnosis'[42].

The external ethical dilemma

This is a useful introduction to the wider 'external' issues which are at stake here. They resolve, essentially, into the familiar one of 'If it can be done, should it be done?' Again, there is no ethical consensus. The 'external' question addresses the charge made by opponents of some or all such testing, that it represents a quest for the 'perfect baby', often translated into the popular imagery of the doctors playing god. This now merits attention. The core of the ethical dilemma revolves around, first, whether fetuses and embryos are entitled to the same protection and treatment as other people, such that the appropriate standards to be applied to their care are those equivalent to those established in *Re B* and *Re C*. Secondly, the question follows, if fetuses, embryos and other human beings are not fully com-parable, whether it still amounts to discrimination against handicapped people genetically to engineer the embryo or abort the handicapped fetus.

For some people, the argument that fetuses should be aborted on any grounds is morally unthinkable. Others hold that abortion on any grounds is permissible at the request of the pregnant woman. Others hold that the interests of the state, whether in the genetic pool, or in the demands made on the Treasury by handicapped people, entail the compulsory screening for genetic disease and handicap and the enforced sterilisation of affected individuals in order to ensure that they do not procreate. My task in this section will be to try and discover on what principle the goal of prenatal genetic screening and diagnosis can justify the abortion of genetically-damaged fetuses and the non-treatment of severely-handicapped neonates and yet be defended against the charge that this discriminates against the handicapped.

One possibility is to consider the fetal interests argument. Here, we are drawn to a distinction made by Ramsey between abortion and fetal euthanasia[43]. The right to live an intolerable and painful existence or to choose to die is one which should be accorded to a fetus as much as to a neonate or to an adult. It follows from this, as Mason has pointed out, that the claim for wrongful life, denied in *McKay*, should be available to the child wrongly forced to live, as much as to its parents, wrongly forced to care for the child[44]. This much is straightforward. The enormous difficulty to which this fetal interests argument gives rise is the increasing recognition of the fetus as a legal person independent of its mother. The dangers of doing this are rehearsed elsewhere[45], and I believe that this conclusion should be avoided.

The fundamental issue at stake in this external argument is whether therapeutic abortion on the grounds of fetal handicap or abnormality discriminates in an objectionable way against handicapped people generally, and whether it enforces a view about 'acceptable' babies and people. The 'therapy' applied in these cases eliminates the disorder by eliminating the patient. But to deny, as we rightly should, that a handicapped person *necessarily* will have a less fulfilled life, does not mean that we are committed to the view which adduces no grounds for preferring the birth of a normal child to a handicapped one. As Glover has pointed out[46] if we conceive of a case in which we deliberately cause a child to be born handicapped, most would consider this a 'monstrous' thing to do. It does not commit us to saying that handicapped children or adults are less worthy of respect or love or care to say that we may rightly choose to produce a child who is not handicapped rather than one who is. And, as Ruth Chadwick has noted, the important boundary is not that between the handicapped and the healthy, but between fetuses and adults. It is not the case that only handicapped fetuses are aborted, for healthy fetuses are similarly dealt with if they constitute a threat to the health or welfare of the mother. 'The thinking behind eugenic abortion is not necessarily that genetically handicapped people are less valuable in some overall sense than others. The idea may be that fetuses are not yet people and we are still in some sense deciding what sort of child to have.'[47]

It seems to be the case that all things being equal, we do indeed have a preference for being born without a handicap than with a handicap. If it makes sense for people to see death as being in their interests, there is a parallel possibility of parents or doctors thinking that not being born at all may be in the interests of a potential child. One difficulty with this analysis, of course, is that the grounds for so thinking may vary, from those which are very narrowly drawn, i.e. serious genetic disease or handicap, to those which are very widely drawn, such as parental unfitness (howsoever defined) to raise and care for the child.

Glover provides what is, in my view, a promising way forward. The difficulty, he adduces, in identifying what harm a handicapped person has suffered by being born with a handicap rather than not at all misses a vital component:

... reproductive ethics seems to be a field in which there are 'impersonal' harms and benefits. Harm can be done without there being identifiable people who are worse off than *they* otherwise would have been. In explaining why it is better to avert the conception of someone with a severe medical condition, we can use the idea of impersonal harms, without having to resort to metaphysical claims about benefits to a particular non-existent person[48].

To be sure, this does not answer all the questions, for it requires us then to decide what sorts of handicap and disability are sufficiently grave to justify entertaining the notion that it is preferable for no person to be born at all than a person with this given handicap. In these circumstances, it seems to me it is then part of what being a human parent is about that this particular decision should be left to the individuals concerned, with the advice and support of their medical carers to make such a personal, perhaps even individual, reproductive decision.

The more distant issues concern forms of genetic engineering which can produce particular genetic features for individuals. The European Parliament has argued that there is a right 'to genetic inheritance which has not been artificially interfered with, except for therapeutic purposes'[49]. Again, as Glover has convincingly argued, those whose genes had been altered to make them more intelligent or attractive might not feel that a right which they had had been interfered with, or indeed if it had that they had been deleteriously interfered with; 'there is a suspicion that the "right" has been plucked out of the air to settle a difficult issue at great speed'[50]. The vast ethical questions raised by positive genetic engineering are outwith the scope of this paper. For the present, only the following, inconclusive, comment is offered.

The problems of technological risk (accidents), governmental control (and potential for abuse), the frequent selection of certain characteristics and the potential for discrimination against those not so selected, and the difficulties of deciding who should make decisions of positive genetic engineering are thought by some to be of sufficient weight to ensure the ethical dubiety of such engineering, whatever its potential benefits[51]. As Bernard Williams has pointed out, there are deep questions of personal identity involved with genetic engineering, especially where its use is contemplated in the state directed eugenic sense; 'we might well wonder *who were* the people'[52]. We may well have learned enough in the last 150 years to believe that positive genetic engineering is too fraught with difficulties and danger presently to be contemplated.

PART II

FETAL SEX IDENTIFICATION, ABORTION AND THE LAW

Reproductive technologies have forced many difficult and pressing questions on to the social and legal agendas. One of the most contested is the use of different techniques for the purposes of sex selection or sex-predetermination of intended children. Media reports over the last four years have highlighted the existence of a number of controversial practices; in this part of the paper, I want to concentrate on the use of sex-determination for the purpose of selective abortion of female fetuses.

How prevalent is sex selection?

In January 1988, the *Today* radio programme carried a report, shadowed in *The Independent* and *The Guardian*[53] of Asian and Middle Eastern women seeking abortions following amniocentesis tests which disclosed that the fetuses which they were carrying were female. One estimate has suggested that up to 100 abortions each year are performed in the United Kingdom on this ground alone, but the figure is very difficult to verify. What can be confidently stated is that the practice is much more widespread, particularly among Indian and Asian communities, than has been thought or acknowledged, and that if the abortion cannot be achieved in this country, women fly to India, on a prearranged package, for the abortion. In an article called 'The Mania for Sons' Ramanamma and Bambawale published their investigation of two hospitals in India where in the late 1970s amniocentesis had been used for the selective abortion of female fetuses. Of 400 women consulting one hospital in 1976–1977, 92 were prepared to indicate that their reason for wanting to know the sex of the fetus was for the purposes of termination if it were female. At the other hospital, of 700 women attending the hospital in one year, 450 were told they were carrying a female fetus, of which 430 aborted[54].

Traditionally, the Chinese have believed that only a son can worship ancestors and continue a family line. Evidence offered by the *Washington Post* in 1985 suggested that 300 000 cases of infanticide occurred in 1982 and 345 000 in 1983. In 1983, the *People's Daily* reported that 'At present the phenomenon of butchering, drowning and leaving female babies to die is very serious.' In one report, Mirsky suggested that the registration of birth figures disclosed that up to 20% of female infants were being killed[55]. Similarly, Colin Thubron's reportage of his Chinese journey records accounts of female infanticide:

> [Being sold off as a young bride] was better than being killed in infancy. I heard of them being killed in other villages. It was quite common. The peasants would just drop them into the water and drown the.... You see, they don't think. They just drop it in. They just say 'It's a girl! It's worthless!' Girls are not *descendants*, you understand. They're not viewed that way. It's boys who continue our line[56].

> It's wrong to limit babies. I've heard about these one-child families in the towns, and the children growing up to be little emperors. Spoilt. And what do you do if you only have a girl? Confucius said your first duty was to give your parents heirs— to carry on the name. It's terrible to have no son. People die out that way.... I said: 'so what happens to the girl babies?' But I knew, of course, what sometimes happens. The custom of killing them is inveterate. In the last century missionaries often came upon baby girls, sometimes still alive, pitched over town ramparts to the rubbish and pariah dogs below. The man said: 'Occasionally girl babies are abandoned on the town streets, and people adopt them. There's no penalty attached to adopting. But out here everyone wants sons. Girls can't do the same heavy work.... So, sometimes, secretly, the girl babies are drowned[57].

Abortions on such grounds as fetal sex are said to be in direct conflict with advice tendered in a Department of Health & Social Security letter of 17.12.1985, that such abortions in the United Kingdom would not be protected by the terms of Section 1 of the Abortion Act 1967. That letter, sent to all proprietors of nursing homes registered under the Act, was prompted by similar allegations made in an 'Eastern Eye' London Weekend Television programme earlier that year, taken up by the *Daily Mail*[58]. In May 1986, the *Sunday Times* carried an article purporting to disclose further abuses of the Act[59], and the American-based weekly, *Time*, highlighted the prevalence of sex pre-selection as a gathering alternative to female infanticide in India, China and South East Asia, where, in all but the most remote provinces, infanticide has been curbed[60].

The mania for sons

Son-preference has roots implanted as firmly in Western as in other cultures. The surviving extent of son-preference in Western societies helps to explain the importance of the issues being addressed here. Many surveys have concluded that women express more disappointment about having daughters than sons, when this information is acquired *at birth*. In 1954 Dinitz, Dynes and Clark reported that 62% of the males surveyed and 58% of the females expressed a preference for a firstborn son, with the respective percentages increasing to 92% and 66% if the question related to the sex of an only-born child. Only 4% expressed a desire for a firstborn daughter. By 1971, a similar survey revealed male/female preferences of 80% and 79% for a firstborn son and 12% for a daughter, and in 1984 a survey response of

62% expressed a preference for a son compared with 6% for a daughter[61].

Research reported in 1983, since the more public advent of reproductive technologies, has tended to reinforce these earlier findings. Respondents were asked whether, if the technology were available, they would avail themselves of sex predetermination techniques. Of those replying 'yes' 81% of the women and 94% of the men preferred firstborn sons. It is instructive to compare these preferences with those disclosed by women who are themselves pregnant. In 1971 an American survey (a 46% son preference, a 32% daughter preference and a 22% no preference) discovered no statistical difference amongst 81 women pregnant for the first time. Similarly, a British study in 1978 conducted by Ann Oakley revealed figures of 54%, 22% and 25% among pregnant women and a further study in 1984 has recorded figures of 25%, 7% and 48%, respectively.

In 1983, one study for the first time demonstrated a preference for firstborn girls. Surveying 140 women pregnant for the first time, and in the last three months of their pregnancies, it suggested that, of those expressing a preference for the sex of their baby, 57% would choose to have a firstborn girl. Three hypotheses to explain this finding are suggested:

(i) that American society is becoming less biased, and that male and female infants are equally highly valued;

(ii) that women actually have an underlying preference for girls, and that the research has managed to detect this;

(iii) that expectant mothers in the 1980s, aware of the cultural thrust towards equality, are reluctant to make inappropriate looking choices and express sexual stereotypes in their questionnaire responses[62].

The tenor of these findings is reflected in an independent study by Barbara Katz Rothman[63]. Of 50 women learning the sex of their babies following amniocentesis, 10 expressed disappointment. All were carrying male babies. Rothman's conclusion, having adjusted for factors which might have influenced these women's desires, was that 'It's one thing to have given birth to a son. It's another to be told that the fetus growing inside your body is male. . . . To have a male growing in a female body is to contain your own antithesis. It makes of the fetus not a continuation and extension of self, but an "other"[64].'

These differing research findings suggest, then, that we must approach with caution presenting reasons for abortion following the identification of fetal sex. Whose reasons for wanting the abortion are we really considering, and what factors should and may lawfully be taken into account?

What is the ambit of the Abortion Act 1967?

Recall that the operative section of the present Abortion Act in England and Wales, section 1, provides that no abortion offence is committed when a pregnancy is terminated by a registered medical practitioner if two such doctors in good faith form the opinion that '(a) ... the continuance of the pregnancy would involve risk to the life of the pregnant woman, or of injury to the physical or mental health of the pregnant woman or any existing children of her family, greater than if the pregnancy were continued'.

In assessing the risk to which s.1(1)(a) refers, s.1(2) provides that 'account may be taken of the pregnant woman's actual or reasonably foreseeable environment'. I want to suggest here that those provisions quite clearly can be used to demonstrate the *legality* of abortion following the identification of fetal sex. In so doing, it needs to be clarified that I am not presently concerned with abortions performed following the disclosure of a mental or physical fetal abnormality such that there is a substantial risk that the fetus will be born seriously handicapped, as additionally provided for in s.1(1)(b), which I discussed in Part I.

Three separate factors persuade me of this view. First, the Act, as drafted, allows for termination if it can be shown that the risk to the pregnant woman's health is greater if the pregnancy is allowed to continue compared with the risks attendant on termination. As abortion technology has become more and more sophisticated, the risks associated with its use have fallen, to the point where the risks of serious injury to or death of the pregnant woman are lower in almost all abortions, but particularly early abortions than the risk of death in childbirth[65]. The comparative risk balance of s.1(1)(a) now offers more protection to the pregnant woman.

The second reason relates to the risk of 'injury to the physical or mental health of the pregnant woman [taking account of her] actual or reasonably foreseeable environment'; ss.1(1)(a) and (2). The Act does not suggest that the source of the risks to the pregnant woman's mental or physical health must be the pregnancy itself. It is sufficient that the continuance of the pregnancy is more likely to expose her to those risks than its termination. Indeed, it is widely accepted that s.1(2) permits a wider range of factors affecting the health of the woman to be taken into account than the pregnancy[66]. The fact that the termination will relieve those risks does not affect the legality of performing the operation for those reasons. The Act does not attempt to limit the source of the risks to which the woman might be exposed; '... it is really quite clear that the Act is intended to provide for the overburdened mother'[67]. The threat to her physical or mental well-being by virtue of the fact of the hostility which the birth will occasion is demonstrably within the scope of the section.

Finally, the Act additionally provides that an abortion may be performed 'where the continuance of the pregnancy would involve risk ... of injury to the physical or mental health of ... any existing children of her family, greater than if the pregnancy were terminated'. In families where existing female children are already regarded as a financial, social and cultural burden the addition of yet another female child might not only deleteriously affect the woman and the child she is then carrying, but also those existing children. Each successive child may become a greater burden on the family's purse, prestige and power. Termination in such circum-stances may, at least, be arguable to safeguard the physical and mental health of the woman's present children; this might be thought the arguable ground.

I have been concerned in this section not with the ethics of abortion on the grounds of fetal sex, but with its legality. Contrary to the advice tendered to the DHSS in 1985 and circulated to registered abortion clinics, I have suggested that the abortion of a healthy fetus on the grounds of its sex alone is permissible under the Abortion Act 1967.

REPRODUCTIVE ETHICS: THE SEARCH FOR THE PERFECT SOCIETY?

When the Warnock Committee presented its report in 1984, they evidenced a number of potential uses to which the existing and developing techniques of sex-selection might be put, and some of the consequences of such usages. Paralleled with the development of reliable and simple sex-prediction tests which can be self-administered before fertilisation, they recommended that the 'whole question of the acceptability of sex-selection should be kept under review'[68]. The Government White Paper, *Human Fertilisation and Embryology: A Framework for Legislation*[69] makes no reference to sex-selection. Warnock resiled from making any recommendations on the control of sex-selection techniques beyond this general overview, however, because 'of the difficulty of predicting the outcome of any such trend'[70]. They did feel dubious about their usage on a wide scale, however, because of the negative image of women which use of the techniques would continue to promote; existing evidence which establishes the benefits which first born siblings enjoy over later children; and the unknown effects on the ratio of males to females.

What is wrong with gender selection? John Harris has argued that it could be used, along with methods of artificially-inducing parthenogenesis, to produce an all-female society in which the inhabitants were all like their mothers, to the extent that genetic differences had not been engineered in[71]. But Harris is in the minority in thinking that this is how gender selection would in fact work. Edward Yoxen, reviewing some of the demographic data available has concluded that if sex predetermination were practised on any scale in Western societies, the population ratio would not shift significantly, that there would be fewer families of all boys or all girls, but that fewer girls would be first born children[72]. Ruth Chadwick has surveyed different accounts of the effects of gender choice and the sex ratio, and the fears to which this has given rise. These range from the hypothetical Manland society of Joanna Russ through the apocalyptic vision of Roberta Steinbacher and Helen B Holmes. In the first, Chadwick identifies the self-defeating argument[73]. This proposes that if all women were eliminated from a future society, some men would be assigned female roles. This same point is made in Harris's preview of an all-female society. On the other hand, Steinbacher and Holmes's fears are more immediate: 'However devalued, controlled, feared or exploited women have been, their indispensability to the continuation of the human race has remained a stubborn fact ... now, for the first time in human history, the power is at hand to negate that indispensability ... There is, to be blunt, the possibility of femicide.'[74]

If my argument in Part I, that abortion following the identification of fetal handicap does not *necessarily* entail or lead to discrimination against the handicapped, am I not led to the same conclusion in respect of gender grounds for abortion? There I argued that sometimes sex-selection has a medical justification and, although there is no consensus, can be defended. Do not the same arguments apply here?

I think not. The point of the argument in Part I was that such abortion was justified where it could be shown to be in the interests of the fetus or its mother that it should be relieved of a life that would be a burden *above and beyond that which life imposes on all of us*. Gender selection *simpliciter* carries no such rationale. Although it might be said that abortion on the grounds of gender relieved the fetus of possible infanticide following its live birth, or that abortion relieved its mother of physical and psychological abuse for the production of a female child, these reasons are qualitatively different from those adduced earlier. Indeed, the major objection to such femicide is that it legitimates desires and preferences that we might want to regard as, at best, highly questionable. While such selection would extend the ambit of choice which parents have, we need to look carefully at the preferences involved. Gender is not a disease. There is, as the examples quoted above illustrate, the danger that gender-selection is used to reinforce attitudes of sex prejudice which we might want to work to undermine rather than satisfy. This does, indeed, entail a commitment to denying some parental choices. But we may be prepared to ask precisely what sorts of choice we are committed to if gender selection is one of them. What sort of people are we and what sort of people do we want to become?

At the very least, it may be said that gender selection violates a principle of equality between males and females and the psychological importance to parenting of an unconditional acceptance of a new child by its intended parents. Furthermore, gender selection may become a precedent for genetic tinkering, encouraging parents to select other desired characteristics for their children. Of course, that then leaves us with the problem of how to control, or limit, or, if this we prefer, encourage gender selection. Yoxen has argued that reproductive freedom entails as great a possible commitment to unrestrained choice as possible. But, with gender selection, there is the fear of what 'the values of a possible society' might entail[75]. Nonetheless, he concludes that prohibition encourages only evasion, and that as a responsible society, we need to face the arguments and respond with argument, and not with legislative restriction. Glover reaches the same conclusion; that the desires behind the choice of sex will often be ones society would do better to discourage and that 'our best hope is the erosion of attitudes which make sex choice seem so important[76].

How adequate are these responses? There is a final note which is appropriate to sound here. It too is committed to the search for the perfect society, but it differs from the sort of society in which fetal sex identification is a necessary feature. Individuals living in a society often have little choice. This, indeed lies at the root of fetal abortion on the grounds of sex alone. As Barbara Katz Rothman has put it, the question then becomes, not whether individual choices are constructed, but how they are constructed[77]. It may be that there can never be 'free' unstructured reproductive choice. But we may at least strive to ensure that the structures within which choices are exercised are fair, ethical and defensible ones. If reproductive choice or reproductive autonomy cannot be effectively secured for all members of any culture, how can rules of law and ethics be so structured in order to protect those vulnerable to abuses of the power which the culture stacks against them? Rothman suggests that the 'next step in the politics of reproductive control is the politics of social control'[78]. While individual rights of access to information, such as fetal sex and fetal health, may be necessary for a system in which reproductive choices can be made, they re not a sufficient guarantee that reproductive autonomy has been secured.

REFERENCES

1. Katherine O'Donovan, Sexual Divisions in Law, 1985, p. xi
2. Gordon Rattray Taylor, The Biological Timebomb, 1968, p. 42
3. Royal College of Physicians of London, Prenatal Diagnosis and Prenatal Screening: Community and Service Implications, 1989, §6.13
4. Usually called selective reduction, but properly identified as completely random by Sheila McLean in discussing this issue at the Aberdeen Conference, November 1989
5. See, e.g. the exchange between John Keown 'Why Selective Reduction Could Result in Criminal Proceedings', The Third Report of the Voluntary Licensing Authority, Annex 4 and David Price, 'Selective reduction and Feticide: The parameters of Abortion' [1988] Criminal Law Rev. 199
6. (1986) 321 Nature p. 720
7. Handyside et al., The Lancet, 18 February 1989
8. See N Lench et al., 'Simple non invasive method to obtain DNA for gene analysis', The Lancet, cited RCP Report, supra, note 2, §3.6
9. Interim Licensing Authority, IVF Research in the UK, November 1989
10. RCP Report, supra, note 2, Table 7
11. Ibid, §2.36
12. Ibid, §3.6
13. Ibid, Preface
14. Ibid, §§1.9, 1.11
15. The three levels of ultrasound scanning are discussed, ibid, §§2.13–23
16. Ibid, §§1.17–18; proportion of mothers over 35 fell in 1950 from over 20% to between 6–10% in the mid/late 1970s. Since older women are particularly at risk for Down's syndrome fetuses, and more than 40% of all pregnancies in women over 35 are aborted for social reasons, this has led to a fall of almost 50% in incidence of Down's births and age profile of much younger mothers bearing Downs
17. Ibid, §3.7, emphasis added

18. Ibid, §5.23
19. Ibid
20. See, e.g. the Lane Committee Report on the Working of the Abortion Act 1967, Cmnd 5579, 1974, §211, 'The decision to be made as to an abortion under section 1(1)(b) by the mother and father and the medical advisers may be among the most difficult under the Act, for example where it is known that there is a risk but that it is not of a high order. We do not think that it would be appropriate to try to define this statutory ground more precisely and we make no recommendation with regard to the wording of the subection'
21. [1989] 2 All E R 782
22. [1981] 1 WLR 1421
23. I have discussed this case in more detail in (1989) 53 Bulletin of the Institute of Medical Ethics, 13–18
24. See, e.g. Morgan 'Judges on Delivery' (1988) Journal of Social Welfare Law 197, discussing Re F (in utero) [1988] 2 All E R 193, see also R v Tait [1989] 3 All E R 682, although the reasoning in this latter case cannot be defended
25. Ibid
26. I have reviewed this data and the arguments to which they give rise with Celia Wells in 'Medicine, Money, Morals and the Newborn' (1989), Journal of Social Welfare Law 57 and 'The Chiswick Interview' (1989) 96, B.J. Obs & Gyn
27. See Jonathan Glover et al., Fertility and the Family: The Glover Report on Reproductive Technologies to the European Commission, 1989, at p. 101
28. Glanville Williams, Textbook of Criminal Law, 2 ed. 1983, at p. 297
29. Ibid, p. 298
30. RCP Report, supra note 3, §8.5
31. That the English courts have already been seized of the difficulties to which such a formulation might give rise is apparent from Paton v BPAS [1978] 2 All E R 987 and C v S [1987] 1 All E R 1230
32. Draft Recommendations on Prenatal Genetic Screening, Prenatal Genetic Diagnosis and Associated Genetic Counselling
33. RCP Report, supra, note 3, §5.8
34. See for example the provisions of the Human Fertilisation and Embryology Bill, cl 29 providing that genetic information held by the proposed Human Fertilisation and Embryology Authority shall be exempt from the subject access provisions of the on Data Protection Act 1984
35. 529 P 2d 55 (1974), 551 P 2d 334 (1976)
36. See X v Y [1988] 2 All E R 648 and W v Egdell (1989) *The Independent* November 10, 1989 for a discussion of the principles involved in sanctioning a doctor's breach of her or his duty of confidence to her or his patient in the wider public interest. Briefly, where a consultant psychiatrist became aware in the course of a confidential relationship, of facts which led him to believe, in the exercise of sound professional judgment to fear that others may take decisions about his patient on the basis of inadequate information, and where he feared that there was a real risk of consequent danger, not mere distaste or discomfort, to the public, he was entitled to take such steps as were reasonable in all the circumstances to make limited communication of that information.)
37. McKay v Essex AHA [1982] QB 1166
38. See Scuriaga v Powell [1979] 123 S J 406; Udale v Bloomsbury AHA [1983] 2 All E R 522; Emeh v Kensington & Chelsea AHA [1985] 1 Q.B. 1012; Thake v Maurice [1986] 1 Q.B. 669; Gold v Harringey [1987] 3 WLR 649. It seems clear that actions for wrongful birth will lie as much against a negligent counsellor as against a negligent doctor; Rawnsley v Leeds AHA (1981) *The Times* 17.11.1981, p. 2
39. Cm 259, 1987, §37
40. Clause 3
41. These questions have been extensively addressed by the Council of Europe, see Council of Europe Assembly Recommendation 934 (1982) and the reports of the relevant committees on scientific research relating to the human embryo, especially the Appendix by Mr Palacios to the report of the Committee on Science and Technology (Doc 5943, 1988) §§45–53
42. RCP Report, supra, note 3, at §3.12
43. see his 'Reference Points in Deciding about Abortion' in J T Noonan, ed., The Morality of Abortion, 1970

44. See 'Abortion and the Law' in Sheila McLean, ed., Legal Issues in Human Reproduction, 1988, at p. 73
45. See the literature footnoted in 'Judges on delivery', supra note 24
46. Glover, supra, note 27, p. 128
47. Ethics, Reproduction and Genetic Control, 1987, p. 111
48. Glover, supra, note 27, p. 132
49. Supra, note 41
50. Glover, supra note 27, p. 139
51. The UK Government has recently established the [Clothier] Committee on the Ethics of Gene Therapy to draw up an ethical framework within which gene therapy may be permitted; see The Independent, 29 November 1989, p. 8
52. In Problems of the Self, 1973, p. 246. For further discussion of these issues see Chadwick, supra, note 47, pp. 119–27; Glover, supra, note 27, pp 137–40; Edward Yoxen, Unnatural Selection, 1986, pp. 137–73
53. 'Unwanted Girls Being Illegally Aborted', The Independent 4 January 1988, p. 2 and 'Doctors helping Asians abort female foetuses', The Guardian, 4 January 1988, p. 3
54. A Ramanamma and U Bambawale, 'The Mania for Sons' (1980), 14B, Social Science and Medicine 107
55. Quoted in Stephen Trombley, The Right to Reproduce: A History of Coercive Sterilisation, 1988, p. 233
56. Behind the Wall, 1988 ed., p. 25
57. Ibid, p. 276
58. Daily Mail, 25 June 1985
59. Mazher Mahmood and Barrie Penrose, 'Doctor Tells Family to Lie to Gain an Abortion', Sunday Times, 11 May 1989, p. 3
60. 'Curse heaven for Little Girls', Time, 4 January 1988, p. 46
61. These surveys are reviewed in Roberta Steinbacher and Helen B Holmes, 'Prenatal and Preconception Sex choice technologies' in Gena Corea, et al., eds., Man Made Woman, 1985, pp. 52–57. And see Barbara Katz Rothman, The Tentative Pregnancy: Prenatal Diagnosis and the Future of Motherhood, 1988 ed, pp. 133–43
62. Ibid
63. Supra, note 61
64. Ibid, pp. 150
65. Williams, supra, note 28, p. 299; J K Mason and A McCall Smith, Law and Medical Ethics, 2 ed., 1987, p. 73 n.7
66. Ibid, p. 301
67. Ibid
68. Cmnd 9341, 1984, §9.11
69. Cm 259, 1987
70. Ibid
71. See The Value of Life, 1985, pp. 166–73
72. Yoxen, supra, note 52, p. 113
73. Chadwick, supra, note 47, p. 128
74. 'Sex Choice: Survival and Sisterhood' in Gena Corea et. al., supra, note 61
75. Supra, note 52, p. 116
76. Supra, note 27, p. 144
77. 'The Meaning of Choice in Reproductive Technology' in Rita Arditti et. al., eds., Test Tube Women, 1984, pp. 32–33
78. Ibid

9. Discussion for section 3

S. A. M. McLean

The capacity to test for sex pre-birth has opened up the possibility that medicine can offer an additional choice to would-be parents. In other words, it may permit couples to choose to continue with a pregnancy where the sex is the desired one or to terminate the pregnancy where it is not. For many, the idea of sex selection is abhorrent. Used on a wide scale it could seriously affect the natural balance of the sexes and seems to diminish the status of the unwanted sex (most probably, female).

These papers concentrate on a number of possible reasons, however, for not condemning the practice out of hand, and Derek Morgan's paper also considers whether or not sex selection is illegal in terms of the Abortion Act 1967. Although reactions to the idea of sex selection may be strong and sometimes hostile, they only touch on some of the issues. The well-documented (although, it is suggested not immutable) preference for first-born sons may be taken as an affront to females. Yet, as Professor Macnaughton points out, for some cultures the birth of a son is a genuinely held cultural desire—some might even say a need. In identifying this, doubt may be cast on outlawing the practice on grounds which seem to take no account of, or pay little respect to, the culture of others. In a pluralistic society, it is arguable that one dominant culture should not be imposed on others. In noting this, Derek Morgan concludes that—where distress can be shown—the terms of s.1 of the Abortion Act 1967 may be met. Thus, he argues, terminating a pregnancy on the grounds of the sex of the embryo/fetus will not necessarily contravene the terms of the legislation. For many, of course, it may remain an ethically dubious practice, but it is in his view not an illegal one if the woman can demonstrate that her mental health will suffer, or that the well-being of any existing children of her family will suffer, as the result of the birth of a child of the unwanted sex.

These social reasons for seeking pregnancy termination are perhaps the most contentious aspects of sex selection, and raise profound ethical questions. Not only do they test the extent to which societies are culturally tolerant, but they also challenge our aspirations for genuine equality of the sexes. These two concepts may ultimately be incompatible, presenting states and individuals with a classic example of the conflict of two 'goods'. As Morgan also points out, there is also the real potential when social grounds are used for reinforcing discrimination based not only on sex (which is biologically determined) but also on the basis of assumptions about gender.

There are, however, additional reasons for wishing to identify the sex of a child before birth. These reasons may broadly be classified as clinical or medical, although they may also be considered to be social. It is a fact of life that certain inherited conditions are carried (but not suffered from) by females, whilst the male will suffer from the condition itself. Families with a high risk of transmitting such conditions may well seek a pre-natal determination of the sex of their child for the reason that they may wish not to have a child which will actually suffer from the relevant condition. For many people, this aspect of sex determination and selection is considerably less objectionable, if it is objectionable at all. The capacity to avoid unnecessary suffering for the subsequent child and the family concerned is routinely viewed as desirable, and where this can be done pre-natally, as opposed to at the neonate stage, it is probably regarded as morally preferable. Certainly, when decisions are based on these grounds it would be hard indeed were pregnancy termination based on the outcome of sex identification not to be legally available pre-natally, given a legal system which would apparently countenance the non-treatment of some of these same children after birth.

Perhaps the most important conclusion reached in discussion of these papers was the extent to which consensus emerged on the matter of counselling. Whilst conceding that there may be acceptable reasons for wishing to identify sex pre-natally, it was strongly felt that the implications of so doing should—as with the detection of other characteristics pre-natally—always be preceded by counselling of the woman and—where relevant—her partner. Counselling was also felt to be vital in the (perhaps more common) situation where the couple already have one affected child and are contemplating embarking on a further pregnancy.

The Warnock Report recommended that the question of sex selection should be kept under review, but made no stronger recommendation than that. Yet—apart from the terms of the Abortion Act 1967 and the media excitement generated by reports of the practice being carried out—there is no clear regulation of this aspect of modern technological capacity. As techniques improve selection may be possible at all stages from conception on. In these circumstances, and given the potential for its use in ethically uncertain situations, it may be time for some regulation to be imposed. However, it is not clear from which source such regulation might come, or how detailed it should or would be. Certainly the Human Fertilisation and Embryology Authority may choose to provide some regulation in respect of those working in artificial reproductive technology, although no specific mention is made of this in the Human Fertilisation and Embryology Bill. However, the practice of sex selection through abortion is less obviously susceptible of regulation, and many may feel that in any event it should not be regulated on the grounds that cultural choices of this sort should be respected.

However, even conceding the value of, and respect owed to, cultural differences, it may not only be on cultural grounds that such decisions are taken. Indeed, if abortion is available to those whose cultural background makes the sex of their children extremely important, it can scarcely be denied to those who might be equally distressed by the birth of a child of the unwanted sex based solely on preference. Moreover, for those to whom the 'slippery slope' argument has appeal, if characteristics such as sex can be permitted to predict the continuation or not of a pregnancy, it might be asked, why cannot other desired characteristics also do so. The argument would, therefore, run that permitting sex selection effectively opens the door to the possibility of choosing 'designer children' on the basis of other desired characteristics, or rather negating the fulfilment of the potential of those who do not meet the desired standard.

It is sometimes said that the unsought for consequences of technological advance may prove to be as problematic as those which are sought. The capacity, developed for sound clinical reasons, to predict sex earlier and earlier, the potential for genetic manipulation and our understanding of inherited disease have also posed (along with their welcome consequences) a serious ethical dilemma and one whose resolution may well confront societies with complex and unforeseen difficulties. That they should be addressed was in no doubt, but on what basis and with what outcome was less clear.

Obstetric litigation

10. Double indemnity and obstetric practice

E. M. Symonds

The definition of indemnity according to the Shorter Oxford English Dictionary is: 'Security against damages or loss; legal exemption from penalties etc. incurred; compensation for loss incurred; sum paid for this, especially sum exacted by victorious belligerent as one condition of peace.'

In obstetrics, we have to indemnify two people at once—the mother and the baby. Furthermore, problems with a newborn child must envisage many years of active support and whilst life expectancy may be limited in cases of severe brain disorders, the costs are cumulative and high even without an imponderable sum allocated for pain and suffering. Furthermore, the costs are enhanced by the fact that any individual who is deemed to have suffered harm from the activities of medical and nursing staff in the National Health Service is entitled to costs equivalent to full care in the private sector. Two major changes have been seen in the last decade. The first has been the substantial increase in the number of claims in all disciplines but in particular in obstetrics. The Medical Defence Organisations have not released actual figures of claims initiated in each discipline but information from the Medical Defence Union suggests that the number of claims has risen from approximately 600/year in 1983 to 1600/year in 1988. What is certain, and has been published, is that the cost of settlement has increased substantially. For example, the data released by the Medical Protection Society[1] in relation to settlements for failed sterilisation show the extent of increase in gynaecological cases where settlement has risen from £1000 in 1976 to £39 964 in 1986. The information in relation to settlements for brain damage shows that within 10 years there has been a ten-fold increase in the maximum settlement, from £130 000 to £1 300 000. I do not know the precise increase in the cost of living or in salaries over that decade but I cannot believe that it is a ten-fold increase.

Proof of overall increases in indemnity payments are not difficult to find. In Figure 10.1 is shown the actual value of indemnity payments during the 1980s, as well as legal charges and disbursements. These data are derived from the annual reports of the MDU. The figures have risen from £2 000 000 to £25 000 000 over a period of 8 years. Note also the parallel increase in legal fees and additional disbursements for expert opinions. These figures actually exceed the sums of money paid to the plaintiffs in

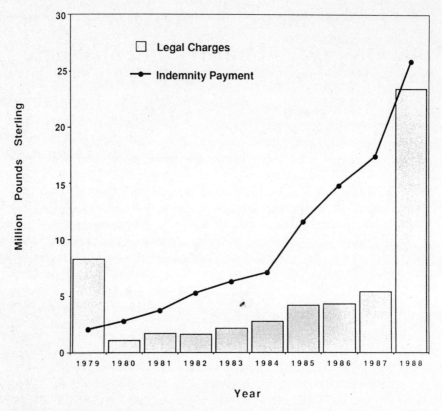

Fig. 10.1   Indemnity payments and legal charges and disbursements derived from annual reports of the Medical Defence Union (1979–1988).

cases of medical negligence. Further evidence of the increasing costs of medical indemnity can be seen by examining the income and subscription charges since 1979 (Fig. 10.2).

It is important to remember that there is a long period for claims on brain damage where this is related to the birth process. This introduces some imponderable factors in assessing the present rate of increase in indemnity payments. There are no published data at the present time to indicate how long after birth legal action is being initiated. We do know that claims are being settled that relate to deliveries more than 20 years ago. We also know that there are many claims that are arising from recent events because the awareness of claim settlements has been considerably enhanced by the publicity given to these events. The current estimate suggests that up to 400 new claims per year are being initiated on the basis of cerebral damage related to the birth process. It is not certain how many cases will emerge in the future from previous problems when the 'latent' claims eventually emerge. The impact of these claims is already being seen and it would not be

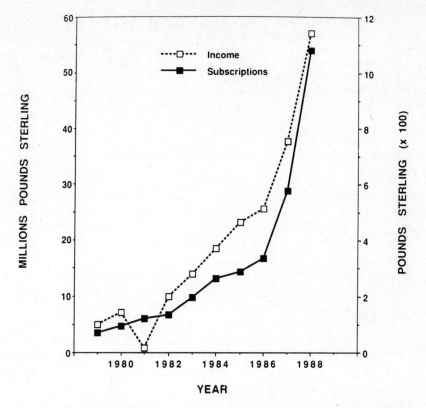

Fig. 10.2 Subscription charges and subscription income of the Medical Defence Union (1979–1988).

inappropriate to remind current practitioners of the fine art of obstetrics that, theoretically, they may be asked to appear in the witness box as a defendant at the age of 90 years, given the possibility that they last that long and that the claim has to join a long queue of 4 years before it reaches the Courtroom!

The introduction of Crown indemnity has followed as a direct result of this dramatic escalation of costs related to obstetric practice, but for reasons that shall be enumerated later in this paper, this step is unlikely to resolve the difficulties.

THE NATURE OF CLAIMS FOR THE 'BRAIN-DAMAGED' INFANT

In 1987, as a member of the Council of the Medical Defence Union, I prepared 102 medico-legal reports. In the absence of any global figures for the Medical Defence Union, I felt that it may be of some interest to share

Table 10.1 Method of delivery in claims for
birth related injuries

31 consecutive cases reviewed	
Forceps delivery	9
Failed forceps—Caesarean section	8
Caesarean section in labour	7
Spontaneous vaginal delivery	5
Breech delivery	1
Shoulder dystocia—vaginal delivery	1

with you some of the details of these claims, particularly because they
encompass the major problems that we now see repetitively in allegations of
negligence in the management of obstetric cases. Of the allegations that
relate to brain damage, 31 appeared in my files. There were, of course,
many claims for failed sterilisations and various other gynaecological
problems, but as these claims are generally of low cost, they do not distort
the general pattern of litigation costs, even if they do generate considerable
tension and anxiety amongst the parties involved.

If we concentrate on the brain damage claims, Table 10.1 shows the
methods of delivery.

The first thing that is evident is that litigation may occur regardless of the
method of delivery. If the child is delivered by forceps or ventouse then the
claim is usually based on the premise that the instruments caused the
damage or that intervention was too late. Unfortunately, intervention is
often based on the presence of fetal distress. So if the obstetrician performs
a forceps delivery for fetal distress and the outcome is unsatisfactory, i.e.
the child is subsequently shown to be mentally retarded or to have cerebral
palsy, then the obstetrician may expect to receive a claim of negligence.
Should there be intervention by Caesarean section, then the allegation will
read that intervention was too late and that had the Caesarean section been
performed earlier, this damage would never have occurred.

The worst of all worlds occurs when an attempt is made to deliver the
child by forceps which fails and delivery by Caesarean section is required.
In this situation, as occurred in Whitehouse vs Jordan and the West
Midlands Health Authority, the claim can always be made that cephalo-
pelvic disproportion should have been anticipated and that damage resulted
from prolonged asphyxia or from cerebral trauma resulting from the
attempted forceps delivery.

Finally, if spontaneous delivery occurs, it is always possible to find some
abnormality in the CTG which can be used as an argument to allege that
earlier intervention should have been initiated and that had this been the
case, the child would undoubtedly be normal with full intellectual
potential. The reality is that the birth process is important in only about
10% of all cases of cerebral palsy.

THE ABNORMAL CARDIOTOCOGRAPH

Probably the biggest single disaster inflicted upon obstetricians and midwives from a medico-legal point of view has been the continuous record of the fetal heart rate in labour. Unlike any other intensive care situation, we keep a record of the fetal heart rate enshrined in a paper record. I want you to speculate for a moment about the interpretation of management of a neonate who was subjected to continuous heart rate monitoring and where the subsequent outcome was analysed in relation to that information, retrospectively.

Given that sensitivity is high and specificity is low, the situation is exemplified by the tracing shown in Figure 10.3. Profound decelerations which persisted for many hours (Fig. 10.4) and a conservative Registrar who chose to believe normal scalp blood acid-base measurements and to persist with conservative management meant the spontaneous vaginal delivery of a healthy infant with a cord artery pH of 7.27 and a one minute Apgar score of 9.

If you examine this tracing, you can decide that the normal heart rate pattern between decelerations means that the tracing is normal. However, if the child had been abnormal at birth and had subsequently shown signs of cerebral palsy, the plaintiff's expert could no doubt advise the Judge that this tracing was abnormal and even if this was directly contradicted, the Judge would be likely to favour the plaintiff's case where there was an abnormal outcome associated with an abnormal tracing.

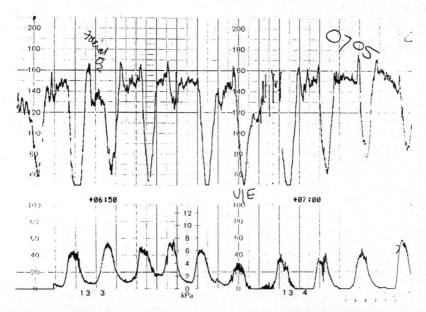

Fig. 10.3 Cardiotocograph in the first stage of labour showing profound heart rate decelerations during labour.

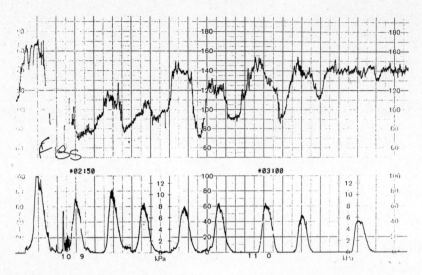

Fig. 10.4   Further CTG recording in the same fetus at the end of the first stage of labour.

The message is that the obstetrician would do well to carry out Caesarean section on any mother where the fetal heart rate is abnormal rather than adopt a conservative stance, irrespective of the logic of any contrary argument. Furthermore, if there is a feeling that it would be better not to monitor at all, there is always the risk of legal action because of the failure to monitor.

MULTIPLE PREGNANCY

All obstetricians and midwives know that life for a second-born twin is always more hazardous than for the first twin. Yet an increasing number of claims are now emerging related to the management of second twins. Recently a settlement was announced in the case of Wakeham versus the Exeter Health Authority. This was a judgment that forms something of a landmark in obstetric litigation and it bears time to consider the implications. The plaintiff was born some 20 years ago and the action was not initiated until the 'child' was 17 years old.

The mother was admitted to hospital on a Saturday in suspected premature labour. Initially, nothing very much appeared to happen but late on Saturday afternoon the cervix became fully dilated and unexpectedly the mother suddenly pushed out the first twin. The resident doctor was called. His total experience was limited to some 3 months in obstetrics so he called the Registrar. The Registrar was on call for 3 units in the town—all some distance apart—but the SHO could not locate him. The SHO, realising his limitations, therefore called the Consultant (now deceased) as he did not feel competent to deal with an abnormal lie in a second twin. By the time the

Consultant had arrived some 50 minutes in all had elapsed and there had been a small intrapartum haemorrhage.

The woman was given a general anaesthetic and an internal version and extraction of the second twin by the breech was performed. The Apgar score was 5 at 1 minute and the plaintiff's barrister put forward the argument (supported by one paediatrician) that the damage was due to negligent management with an undue delay (70 minutes) in delivery of the second twin. Two expert neonatologists said there could be no certainty about the aetiology of the cerebral palsy. The plaintiff's expert said that an Apgar score of 5 was a sign of severe fetal asphyxia. He was not a neonatologist and the Judge chose to believe him. On appeal, the original judgment was upheld and one Judge stated that, effectively, the Health Authority had a responsibility to provide effective cover and that the fact that it happened nearly 20 years ago and that the aetiology of the cerebral palsy was uncertain was irrelevant. An award was made of £750 000.

CONCLUSIONS

Unless some form of no fault compensation for birth related injury is introduced soon, two things must inevitably follow: there will be increasing acceptance and belief that all adverse outcome must be the fault of the birth attendant; and there will be, and there is already, increasing difficulty in persuading anyone to accept a role in maternity services.

REFERENCES

1. Briefing Paper 6, Medical Negligence, Compensation and Accountability. Ham C, Dingwall R, Fenn P and Harris D, Centre for Socio-Legal Studies, Oxford, King's Fund Institute, 1988

11. Particular features of obstetric cases

A. Cameron

Obstetric cases are not uncommonly the subject of litigation and only too often, the value of the claim is very large indeed. Whether it is just my own experience or not I cannot say, but in the last two or three years, I have had an increasing number of these cases and they have presented something of a pattern in that they have revealed similar weaknesses from the point of view of defending the treatment and care given to the patient.

I thought I would illustrate what I have to say by reference to three cases with which I have had to deal in the last year. They are typical examples of the kind of case that I have mentioned.

The facts of each case are somewhat involved, not surprisingly, but if I take a little time to set them out, you will see clearly what I mean when I said they presented something of a pattern. You will also see, I am sure, the questions that arise.

In case 1 the mother was a 26-year-old *prima gravida*. She had had an essentially uneventful ante-natal history and was admitted to hospital four days after her expected date of delivery because of suspected spontaneous rupture of the membranes. It was not clear whether the membranes had in fact ruptured but spontaneous uterine activity continued during the night after her admission. At 09:55 hours on the next day (I shall call that day 2), a vaginal examination showed the cervix to be 2 cm dilated with intact forewaters. These were ruptured to encourage uterine activity. At mid-day, an epidural anaesthetic was inserted to provide pain relief and shortly after this an intravenous infusion of Syntocinon was started to stimulate uterine contractions. This infusion of Syntocinon continued for most of the rest of the labour, although it was turned down at points where it was thought that the uterus might be over stimulated. Similarly, throughout the day on a number of occasions, variable decelerations were recorded in the fetal heart rate. Dilatation of the cervix proceeded very quickly until about 8 cm when some arrest occurred. With further stimulation, the cervix became fully dilated and the mother reached the second stage of labour. There was, however, no descent of the presenting part and, after discussion with the Consultant on call, the mother was taken to the operating theatre for an attempted forceps delivery by the Registrar on call. The attempted forceps delivery was carried out by the Registrar under the Consultant's supervision and no descent of the baby's head occurred. Immediately after this, the baby's heart rate was noted to be very slow and the Consultant did an emergency Caesarean section under general anaesthesia, the forceps delivery having been conducted under an epidural anaesthetic. On opening the abdomen, it appeared that the lower segment of the uterus, through which the baby would normally have been delivered, had already ruptured or was in the process of rupturing. A grossly asphyxiated baby was delivered. The damage to the uterus extended down to the cervix and the vaginal vault. This was repaired by the Consultant and a blood transfusion was given. Unfortunately the baby died at the age of 5 days.

That is the unhappy story in brief. Now let us look at it in a little more detail to see what went wrong and why. For this, we have to go to the contemporaneous notes. First, the notes made by members of the medical staff. As is unfortunately the case on so many occasions, these were woefully inadequate. The House Officer noted that, at 09:55 hours, he found the cervix to be 2 cm dilated and at this point ruptured the membranes. Then there is a note to the effect that at 13:30 hours, the cervix was 4–5 cm dilated with the head 1 cm above the ischial spine. At this point the House Officer was able to apply an electrode to the baby's scalp in order to record the fetal heart. That note by the House Officer is the last medical comment on the labour until 02:00 hours the following morning (day 3), that is to say twelve and a half hours later. The note then is written by the Registrar on call. He summarises the facts of the latter part of the labour when, at the time of writing, the mother had been in the second stage of labour for 3 hours. The Registrar notes that there has been no descent of the presenting part and records the presence of 'caput + +'. This means, I understand, oedema and swelling of the baby's scalp. The Registrar notes that the baby feels to be of a large size but says that it was difficult to assess how much of the baby's head is palpable abdominally because of suprapubic tenderness. He also notes that the contractions are becoming less frequent in spite of the Syntocinon infusion and concludes that there is cephalo-pelvic disproportion. He then discussed the case with the Consultant on call and it was he who authorised the attempt at forceps delivery in theatre, ready to proceed to Caesarean section.

For an account of the crucial 12 hours between lunch time on day 2 and the writing of the notes to which I have just referred, we have to turn to the nurses' Kardex. These notes indicate grounds for some anxiety throughout this period. It is not always easy to confirm the nurses' observations about the baby's heart rate by reference to the Cardio-Tocographic tracings, because not all of these tracings have identifying dates and times. Nevertheless, occasional decelerations of the fetal heart are noted at 14:15 hours and again at 14:50 hours when the heart rate had dropped to 70 per minute. At 16:00 hours, the Sister notes late decelerations, a particularly ominous finding. At 17:20 hours, the cervix is recorded at 7 cm dilated. At 17:36 hours, the Syntocinon infusion was switched off because the uterus was hypertonic. At 17:40 hours, the base line rate of the fetal heart is noted to be between 100 and 105. At 18:30 hours, an infusion containing 10 units of Syntocinon (a higher concentration) was commenced. By 19:30 hours, the cervix is 8 cm dilated but the baby's head is still 1 cm above the ischial spine. A repeat vaginal examination at 20:50 hours by the Registrar showed no change in the cervix. Around this time, there was a persistent deceleration recorded on the CTG trace. There is a similarly prolonged deceleration at 21:30 hours. Another examination by the Registrar at 22:00 hours showed the cervix still stuck at 8 cm. Following this, the Syntocinon infusion was increased and at 22:55 hours a vaginal examination by a Sister suggested that the cervix was now fully dilated. At 23:20 hours, the Syntocinon was again switched off because of hypertonus. At 01:00 hours on day 3, the Registrar and Sister both examined the mother and the presence of meconium staining (a sign of fetal distress) was noted. The mother was encouraged to push at this stage to produce descent of the baby's head but it was noted that she complained of right-sided pain. The absence of any progress led the Registrar to contact the Consultant, as already noted, at 02:00 hours.

The independent expert opinion was to the effect that there could be no defending the case. In the circumstances, it had to be concluded that the rupture of the uterus was due to over stimulation by Syntocinon in the presence of cephalo-pelvic disproportion. There was little evidence that the Registrar appreciated the extent of the problem before 02:00 hours on day 3. He had apparently spoken with the Consultant about this case when they met some 4 hours earlier (22:00 hours) in the course of dealing with another case. However, he did not communicate great concern at that time. The independent expert considered that he, the Registrar, was open to criticism in this respect because, as already noted, there was some concern about the behaviour of the fetal heart throughout the latter part of the labour and in addition repeated adjustments of the Syntocinon infusion were required because of episodes of hypertonus. This fact together with the apparent reluctance of the cervix to dilate beyond 8 cm should have raised the possibility of a mechanical problem in the Registrar's mind. The independent expert considered that the midwives had done all that was required of them. In short, the failure of the Registrar to recognise signs of impending difficulty in the labour and distress in the fetus and his consequent failure to consult a Consultant earlier amounted in the circumstances to negligence.

In case 2, the mother was a 30-year-old who had had her first child some 2 years earlier. That first child had been delivered by a Caesarean section because of failure to progress in labour and the development of fetal distress. In this second pregnancy, it was decided in the ante-natal period to allow another attempt at vaginal delivery. A few days after the expected date of delivery, she was briefly admitted threatening to go into labour but did not proceed and went home. She was re-admitted some 10 days later at about mid-day (day 1). Progress was slow throughout the day, but the membranes remained intact and the mother remained in an ante-natal ward for part of the day. She was admitted to the labour ward at 22:15 hours on that day, contracting every 3 to 4 minutes. She was noted to be tense and anxious. At 23:00 hours, some type 1 dips in the fetal heart rate were noted in the nurses' Kardex. I understand that these are decelerations of the fetal heart rate occurring early in a contraction and may be of no sinister significance. A vaginal examination was carried out at this time and showed the cervix to be 3 cm dilated. Artificial rupture of membranes was performed and a small amount of what was described as old meconium-stained liquor drained. This, I understand, may be indicative of previous fetal distress and a scalp electrode was applied. It is recorded in the same note that the fetal rate dropped to 108 with contractions and at 23:15, the Senior House Officer on call was notified. The presence of the type 1 dips on the CTG was recorded with the comment that there was good recovery of the fetal heart rate.

Just after midnight, an epidural anaesthetic was inserted and shortly after this a further note by the Registrar on call mentions occasional type 1 dips to about 100 beats per minute with rapid recovery. At 01:20 hours on day 2, because uterine activity was thought to be inadequate, it was stimulated by an intravenous infusion of Syntocinon. A note at 03:00 hours, records the cervix to be 3.5 cm dilated and the fetal heart rate to be 132 and regular but with occasional type 1 dips.

The Consultant on call that night was in the hospital dealing with another problem and saw the mother at 04:00 hours. He noted 'morale is low but epidural is effective and fetal heart satisfactory. Very keen to deliver normally and therefore seems reasonable to continue meantime but if no dramatic change at next assessment she will require repeat Caesarean section.' The Consultant was on call throughout the night, of course, but was not consulted further about the labour. At 06:00 hours, the presence of 'marked' meconium staining was recorded. At 06:50 hours, the mother complained of pain over her previous section scar and the Syntocinon infusion was stopped. The bladder was catheterised and a quantity of urine obtained with apparent improvement in the mother's discomfort. A vaginal examination at this time showed the cervix to be 8 cm dilated. Fetal heart rate appeared to be normal and the Syntocinon infusion was recommenced. A vaginal examination at 09:00 hours by the Registrar coming on duty showed the cervix to be fully dilated with the baby apparently in an occipito-anterior position. Following this, deep type 1 decelerations to 70 beats per minute were noted together with marked meconium staining. The patient was encouraged to push while the Registrar made preparation for a forceps delivery. The delivery note indicates that the base line of the fetal heart rate was 160 per minute with deep decelerations being recorded. The baby's position at delivery was in fact found to be directly occipito-posterior but, as the head was well down in the pelvis, no attempt was made to rotate it and the baby was delivered face to pubis. The baby appeared severely asphyxiated at birth and unfortunately is left with very severe brain damage and consequent handicap.

A proper assessment of this case depended on the CTG tracings. Unfortunately, they made unhappy reading. The trace was in three sections, the first one relating to the period between 20:30 hours and midnight on day 1. From 23:00 hours onwards there was a base line of 130 per minute but reduced beat to beat variation (less than 5 beats per minute). There were also some variable decelerations present and no action was taken. On trace 2, between 00:05 hours and 01:30 hours, the base line was 140. There was very little beat-to-beat variation and there were persistent early decelerations. Again no action was taken. On trace 3, between 01:30 and 03:00 hours the base line was 140. There was poor beat-to-beat variation. There were persistent early decelerations. The only action taken was that Syntocinon infusion was started. At 03:00 hours, the cervix was still 3.5 cm dilated and the Syntocinon infusion was increased. Between 03:00 and 07:00, the base line was 140. There was again poor beat-to-beat variation and persistent early decelerations. Between 07:30 and 09:00 hours, there was no tracing being recorded at all. At 09:00 hours a scalp electrode was re-applied and the cervix was then found to be fully dilated. At that point the base line was 160. There was no beat-to-beat variation and there were persistent prolonged severe early decelerations. Again no action was taken. At 09:30 hours the baby was delivered by Haig Ferguson forceps. From this it can be seen that the CTG tracing from the time the scalp electrode was applied at 23:00 hours was not normal. Those attending the mother were in error in thinking that the 'early decelerations' were benign. The expert advice that we received was that these may be considered benign only in the absence of other obstetric features suggesting asphyxia. These features in this case, however, were present, namely meconium in the liquor and poor beat-to-beat variation in the CTG tracing. Unfortunately, it would appear that all concerned, midwives, Registrar and a Consultant were all in their different ways in the opinion of the independent experts at fault. The medical staff were at fault in misreading the CTG tracing and not taking appropriate action and the midwives were at fault for not monitoring the fetal heart rate at all between 07:30 and 09:00 hours. Again, therefore, the case was indefensible and had to be settled and, as you can imagine, at a very high figure.

In case 3, the mother was aged 28. She had had one previous child and in this pregnancy had had a normal ante-natal history apart from one admission near term after a midwife had thought she had deceleration of the fetal heart. CTG carried out at that time was, however, normal. Some 11 days after her expected delivery date, she was admitted at 02:50 hours in early labour. At 05:00 hours, when contractions were becoming stronger, the Senior House Officer found her on vaginal examination to be 3 to 4 cm dilated and carried out rupture of the membranes when fresh meconium drained. The House Officer applied a fetal scalp electrode and immediately noticed decelerations, but felt they were acceptable at that stage of labour. The patient was given pethidine as an analgesic. At 05:40 hours, the patient was now distressed and, at 05:55 hours, the midwives noted marked deceleration of the fetal heart and apparently informed the Senior House Officer, but the only comment in the midwives' note is that 'the doctor will come to see when free'. In fact, no one came to see the patient and at 06:00 hours, the midwives noted that there was some pressure felt but nothing was visible. No vaginal examination, however, was carried out. At 06:30 hours, the SHO did appear, saw the CTG and the patient and noted a somewhat flat tracing with decelerations. At 07:00 hours there was another large deceleration and the Registrar for the first time was informed. The Registrar saw the patient and the CTG some five minutes later. By this time, the patient was fully dilated and since the baby's head was now visible and the patient had had a baby previously, the Registrar decided that delivery was imminent and encouraged active pushing. The baby was delivered some quarter of an hour later and was flat at birth with much meconium in the airways and stomach. Unfortunately, the baby turned out to be cerebrally damaged.

Once again, the independent expert advice was to the effect that the case was indefensible as the management of the labour and, particularly, the interpretation of a combination of fresh meconium staining and abnormal tracing on the CTG were inadequate. It was considered that responsibility had to be borne to a certain extent by the midwives and to a certain extent by the House Officer because at different times they ought to have recognised that all was not well in the circumstances and sought advice from more senior personnel.

So you see in each case the independent expert advice was that the case was indefensible. And so an out-of-court settlement had to be and was negotiated. It is, of course, sad from everyone's point of view when the outcome is as bad as it was in these three cases but is there anything that we can learn from what happened with a view to reducing the risk of its happening again? For most people involved in those cases it was, I dare say, a one-off experience but when, as I did, you come across three such cases within a few months—and, as I say, they are not the only ones—then it is right to ask a few questions. I do not pretend to be able to give the answers but perhaps the medical men and women among you might be able to do so. For it seems to me that three questions arise out of these cases and they all relate to the training both of medical and nursing staff and to the enforcement of a system that carries that training into practice.

The first question is that of making notes. I realise that this is of general application but in my experience it arises particularly acutely in obstetric cases, perhaps because so much tends to be going on at one and the same time. Now, I well appreciate that we do not want to reach the position where doctors and nurses spend all their time writing notes instead of treating patients. But, if there is a happy medium, then I'm afraid that a complete blank for over 12 hours in medical notes is not it! That perhaps is an extreme example but in very many cases we advocates are presented with notes—and, I have to say, particularly medical notes—that are less than satisfactory, and when that happens the defence of a case is made very much more difficult, if not indeed impossible. The answer to this question may lie in better training but, just as importantly, in insistence by those in charge that a proper standard of note-making be maintained.

The second question is also perhaps of general application but again seems to apply particularly to this type of case. It concerns the failure to call for the assistance of more senior and experienced staff when it is necessary to do so and to take appropriate action if such assistance is not forthcoming sufficiently quickly. Now, I realise very well that such situations are not always easy to deal with for a variety of reasons and are in any event to a great extent judgmental but when the matter is so obviously a matter of life and death, I think that there is a strong case for this being emphasised and insisted on rather more strongly than it often seems to be.

The third question relates particularly to this type of case. That is the teaching and training of both midwifery staff and junior medical staff in the setting up, monitoring and proper interpretation of CTGs in the context of everything else that is going on in labour. I don't know what teaching is given in this technique and I don't know to what extent such teaching is updated but I would suggest that the experience of cases such as these, indicates that there may be room for improvement here.

Now there is not, I think, any connection between these three questions other than that they seem to arise all too frequently in cases of this type. And, as I said, I do not pretend to know the answers to them. But I might tentatively make one suggestion and that is this. When there is an unfortunate outcome such as happened in these cases, there is, I think, an argument for having an in-house inquiry into what happened and whether steps might be taken to try to prevent it happening again. What sort of inquiry it would be would depend upon the circumstances and, of course, such an inquiry might be appropriate not just in obstetric cases but also in many other types of case. I understand that in some hospitals, inquiries of this type do take place but no record is kept of them. That may be an understandable way of dealing with them but is of little long-term usefulness. The advantage of an inquiry of the kind that I have mentioned would be that it would help to identify any points of weakness in the treatment and care given to the patient at a time when events were fresh in everyone's mind, at a time before staff had dispersed to all corners of the globe and at a time when lessons could be learned with immediate and much more telling effect. Such an inquiry would also serve in appropriate cases to show—as often happens but sometimes cannot be shown years later due to inadequate notes, missing records, imperfect recollections or unobtainable witnesses—

that although the outcome was unfortunate, the management of the case was entirely in keeping with accepted medical practice. I am quite sure that the introduction of a procedure such as this would not only be financially beneficial to Health Board and Protection Society alike but would also save patients and their relatives, nurses and doctors a great deal of unhappiness. It would also, I think, do much to increase the regard in which the hospital services and all who work in them are held by the general public—a regard which is rightly already high but which might perhaps be higher still.

I hope that what I have said helps to throw a little light on the type of problem that an advocate is faced with in defending obstetric cases and if anything that I have said helps to bring about a reduction in their occurrence and the unhappiness that they cause, then we will all be delighted.

12. Discussion for section 4

J. M. Watson

Dr J M Watson: Professor Symonds, you have painted a rather gloomy picture indicating that litigation is threatening to wipe out obstetric practice. Can you offer any constructive comments on what could be done to reduce the threat?

Prof Symonds: Obstetricians are in a 'no win' situation. There has been a tremendous and disproportionate increase in obstetrics claims alleging cerebral damage resulting from birth injury. We have inadequate staffing and inadequate funding. Long hours on call are a feature of the NHS. Some problems could be solved tomorrow with adequate staffing levels.

We have had regular audits and reviews in teaching hospitals for many years. The cerebral damage has occurred long before the birth in many cases.

Increasing numbers of cases taken to court are being lost.

I suggest that we take these cases outside the adversarial system and give them support.

Dr J M Watson: Mr Cameron has made three points of relevance:

1. There should be a proper standard of notekeeping.
2. There should be more senior staff called to the labour suite when appropriate.
3. There should be adequate training of medical and midwifery staff regarding CTG traces.

He also made a constructive suggestion that it would be helpful in individual cases to hold an in-house informal inquiry.

Mr Alan Brown: I would like to make some comments about training and supervision. Ten per cent of so-called birth injuries relate to intra-partum problems and paediatricians tell us of them. Ten per cent of them have contributory intra-partum problems. It would help to have more senior people in the labour ward and to have a shift system for supervision and training.

Prof Peter Howie: There could be legal difficulties with an inquiry. Who would initiate it? There would also be problems with confidentiality until the patient made a complaint.

Mr S Simmons: This problem is not due to lack of training or inadequate service in the labour ward. As perinatal mortality decreases, litigation rises. Expectations have gone up. Recruitment into obstetrics is going to be a problem.

Dr Martin Lees: We must account for what we don't understand. People are emotional, not logical and they jump to conclusions. Events are not known for a long time afterwards. A public inquiry would be dangerous but a private inquiry, under these circumstances, would be fine.

Prof A Campbell: The time lag between the incident and a claim arising is a problem. It can't lead to fairness in the system.

Mr Cameron: An inquiry would obviate many of the present difficulties. Doctors have nothing to fear from Scottish judges.

Prof Symonds: This litigation process is going too fast to stop. 'No fault' compensation is the only remedy.

Prof Kenneth Calman: It remains to me as Chairman to thank our two speakers for their excellent papers and Dr Watson for facilitating the discussion.

HIV infection

13. AIDS—medical implications

J. M. Watson

A NEW DISEASE

The appearance of AIDS has created great alarm on a worldwide scale and many think of it as a new epidemic. Despite analogies being drawn between AIDS and other great historic epidemics, AIDS has little in common with these, least of all in the personal risk it seems to pose to doctors generally.

However, many doctors will be faced with patients who want to know if they are infected and others will have patients who present symptoms which make HIV infection part of the differential diagnosis. Many problems associated with patient consent and confidentiality in relation to AIDS have been directed at defence organisations during the last two years.

This paper is written from the standpoint of medical practitioners and examines the ethical and legal aspects of AIDS. The first part is concerned with the law and ethics as they apply in general to patients who are infected or possibly infected with HIV. The next section concentrates on the problems specific to individual obstetric patients. The last part is concerned with the use of ante-natal women to measure the prevalence of the infection in the population.

GOVERNMENT STATEMENTS AND ACTS OF PARLIAMENT

After the test for HIV antibodies became available in 1985, the DHSS recommended that all individuals who wished to be tested should be counselled before having the test and that those who were found to be positive should be counselled afterwards. The importance of strictest confidentiality was also stressed by the DHSS and other bodies[1,2].

AIDS or HIV infection are not notifiable by statute but the following legislation is relevant. All of it applies to England and Wales, but in some cases there is no Scottish equivalent.

The Venereal Diseases Regulations (SI 1974 no. 29) state that every health authority has a statutory duty to ensure that any information capable of identifying persons examined or treated for sexually transmitted diseases shall not be disclosed except to another doctor or to someone employed under the direction of a doctor in connection with the treatment or prevention of the spread of such diseases. The Regulations do not apply to general practitioners or others who are not employed by regional or district health authorities. They are not applicable to Scotland, although the common law duty of confidentiality would be relevant.

The *Public Health (Control of Disease) Act 1984* allows application to be made to a magistrate who may, but is not obliged to, allow the testing for HIV without the patient's consent. The tests must be in the interests of the patient, the family or the public. The provisions of the Act do not cover testing to reassure people, such as policemen or doctors, that they are not at risk[3]. They would not therefore permit testing for HIV for screening purposes. The Act does not apply to Scotland where there is no corresponding legislation.

AIDS is not a notifiable disease in the UK and the Smith Report (1988) clearly recommends that it should not be made notifiable because of the fear that infected patients would not go to a doctor. However, the *Public Health (Infectious Diseases) Regulations 1985* and *Public Health (Infectious Diseases) Regulations 1988* allow a local authority, with the consent of the appropriate health authority, to make an application for the removal to hospital of a person suffering from AIDS and for detention there if there is a risk to other persons. This Act does not apply in Scotland, but the *Public Health (Scotland) Act 1897* would apply. The powers provided by these Acts appear to be rarely used.

The *AIDS (Control) Act 1987* is concerned only with the reporting of statistical information required by the Government.

GENERAL MEDICAL COUNCIL GUIDANCE FOR DOCTORS ABOUT HIV AND AIDS

In May 1987, the General Medical Council issued the interim guidance that doctors who refused to treat a patient who was HIV positive could be charged with serious misconduct. This was based on the duty of doctors always to act in the best interests of their patients.

A statement in August 1988 gave the current guidelines about the care of patients and about doctors who are HIV positive. It also dealt with the general issue of consent to investigation or treatment. 'Doctors are expected in all normal circumstances to be sure that their patients consent to the carrying out of investigative procedures involving the removal of samples or invasive techniques, whether or not those investigations are performed for the purpose of routine screening, for example in pregnancy, or for the more specific purpose of differential diagnosis.' It states that it is particularly important in the case of testing for HIV that patients be given opportunity to consider the implications of the test 'because of the possible serious social and financial consequences which may ensue for the patient from the mere fact of having been tested for the condition'. Only in the most exceptional circumstances where a test is imperative in order to secure the safety of persons other than the patient, and where it is not possible to get the prior consent of the patient, can testing without explicit consent be justified.

The statement also discussed confidentiality and pointed out that most problems about confidentiality in AIDS and HIV cases can be overcome by honest discussion with the patient. If the diagnosis is made by a specialist and, after counselling, the patient insists that his or her GP should not be informed, then these wishes should be respected. The only exception would be if failure to disclose would place the health care team at serious risk. The only valid reason for informing a third party other than another health care professional without the patient's consent would be in the situation where there was a serious and identifiable risk to a specific individual if the information was not given. The Council believed that, after counselling, most patients would agree to their partner being informed but, in the absence of consent, a doctor may consider that it would be required to ensure that a sexual partner was informed regardless of the patient's wishes.

THE BRITISH MEDICAL ASSOCIATION AND AIDS

The BMA has issued statements about AIDS on a number of occasions. Most of these are in broad agreement with the policy of informed consent and confidentiality of the GMC, but at the 1987 BMA Annual Represent-atives Meeting, it was proposed that 'testing for HIV antibodies should be at the discretion of the doctor and should not necessarily require the consent of the patient'. This was very controversial and the proposal was deferred until a legal opinion was sought. This opinion stated that the BMA proposal was likely to be illegal. In July 1988, the Annual Representative Meeting of the BMA accepted the motion that 'HIV testing should be performed only on clinical grounds and with the specific consent of the patient'. This decision was hailed by Dr John Marks, the chairman of the BMA Council, as 'a triumph for common sense'[4].

LEGAL OPINIONS ON HIV TESTING AND CONSENT

Several legal opinions have been obtained about the likely attitude of English law to the matter of testing patients for HIV antibodies. These were given by Mr Michael Sherrard QC and Mr Ian Gatt for the British Medical Association in September 1987, by Mr Leo Charles QC for the CCHMS in May 1988 and by Mr Gordon Langley QC and Messrs Hochhauser and Griffiths for the Medical Defence Union in May 1988. A fourth opinion was obtained in Scotland by the Medical and Dental Defence Union of Scotland in November 1988 from Mr Derek Emslie QC to determine whether there were any significant differences in Scots law. All opinions point out that there is a lack of relevant statute law and previous cases on which to form a clear opinion but all are in general agreement that the testing for HIV antibodies without the consent of the patient would, except for rare circumstances, leave the doctor at risk of both criminal prosecution and civil liability. It is therefore clear that the 1987 BMA resolution could not have been put into practice without risk of severe legal consequences. There are differences between the opinions but these are largely minor in their practical importance.

HIV, CONFIDENTIALITY AND THE COURTS

Confidentiality has usually been regarded in this country as principally a matter of ethics rather than law. However, in a case in 1987, concerning the publication of information taken from the hospital records of two doctors who were being treated for AIDS, Mr Justice Rose decided that the public interest of the confidentiality of medical records of actual or potential AIDS sufferers substantially outweighed the public interest of the freedom of the press. The judge heard six medical experts testify that the most important action for AIDS lay in counselling and that this benefited the public since the patient could be advised about how to avoid placing others at risk. Confidentiality was vital to allow this counselling to be possible. If the patient's confidence was breached, or if the patient feared that it might be breached, the patient would be fearful about coming for counselling[5,6].

This case is important since it illustrates that confidentiality should not be considered to be an absolute right or duty and that, although it was not so in this case, there might be circumstances in which the public interest could justify its breach.

HIV AND OBSTETRICS

The ethical and legal issues of HIV infection and the obstetric patient are exactly the same as for any other patient. Patients should not be tested without consent. They should be counselled adequately before testing and counselled again afterwards if the result is positive.

The Royal College of Obstetricians and Gynaecologists subcommittee on problems associated with AIDS reported in October 1987[7] and subsequently, in March 1988, a RCOG study group on AIDS met to discuss the particular problems of AIDS in gynaecological and obstetrical practice. The papers from the study group have been collected into a volume and provide useful clinical data on all these vital issues[8].

The most obvious problem specific to obstetric patients and HIV is that the fetus has also to be considered. In addition, there are also the problems of the effect of the HIV infection on the outcome of the pregnancy and the possible effects of the pregnancy on the infection. The importance of counselling about HIV infection in pregnancy has therefore been recognised as crucial by obstetricians and others[8,9,10]. One of the main difficulties is that the information given to each patient must not only be tailored to her individual needs but must be current in a field where knowledge is changing rapidly.

An issue of great importance to obstetrics is the question of fetal rights. Could a fetus be made a ward of court if a mother was HIV positive and continued with her harmful life style or could a baby of such a mother be taken into care after delivery? Could a child raise an action against its mother for her reckless behaviour before or during pregnancy which led to the child becoming infected with HIV? Some of these questions have no absolute answers at present since they have not been tested in court. However, in a recent English case[11], not involving AIDS, the Court of Appeal held that an unborn child could not be made a ward of court because the mother's movements would have to be controlled absolutely and this would be too restrictive of her personal liberty. It seems unlikely that the verdict would be different in the case of a mother who was HIV positive. Wardship jurisdiction does not exist in Scotland and there is no similar Scottish case raised on any other ground.

After delivery, a baby can be taken into care by means of a wardship proceedings in England and Wales or by using the Reporter and the Children's Hearing system in Scotland if it can be shown that this is in the best interests of the child. This could only be done on the basis of the mother's life style after the birth of the child.

With regard to the possibility of a child raising an action against the mother, English courts have so far denied the right of action for wrongful life[12]. There is no corresponding Scottish case or statute. In England, a child cannot sue the mother for damages sustained before conception or before birth except for road traffic accidents (Congenital Disabilities (Civil Liability) Act 1976). In Scots Law, there is no such restriction so that an action by a child against the mother is theoretically possible but opinions differ about the likely outcome[13,14].

PREVALENCE TESTING OF ANTE-NATAL PATIENTS

In 1987, Douglas Black, Richard Doll and others pointed out the importance of establishing the prevalence of HIV infection and of monitoring its spread in different groups of the population[15]. They suggested that it would be valuable for this purpose to test all pregnant women for HIV antibodies as a matter of routine. The Smith Report[16], published in 1988, recommended that, as a first step towards the measuring of HIV infection in the general population, there should be screening of ante-natal women but that this should be voluntary, with provision for voluntary unnamed testing. It was thought that the results from this could be extrapolated to the whole population. Various arguments were proposed to justify the testing of ante-natal women. It would be of clinical value to the individual women involved and the cost would be low because blood would be taken for other tests anyway. A well defined population would be tested which would be sensitive to the spread of the disease into the heterosexual population. Ethical objections were raised by some groups, including the Royal College of Midwives, who thought that it was morally wrong to use pregnant women in a surveillance exercise[17].

From the ethical and legal viewpoint, it is essential that the usual principles should be applied to voluntary screening as to the testing of individual patients discussed in the previous sections and that testing should only be performed with specific consent after full counselling about all the risks and benefits. It should be noted by clinicians that the more voluntary the procedure, the more information will have to be given to patients[18]. It is particularly important that patients should be warned about possible complications which might arise with regard to obtaining life insurance after being tested.

A number of surveys of HIV prevalence using volunteer ante-natal patients are at present being carried out in 1989. Nothing has been published yet and results are not available but all are as proposed by the Smith report.

A working group was set up to consider the incidence and prevalence of HIV in England and Wales and resulted in the Cox report[19] which recommended that anonymous testing of the population should be urgently considered. It pointed out that voluntary testing in the USA under-estimated the true prevalence of HIV infection because those who were most likely to be infected were less likely to agree to be tested if given the choice.

In Parliament on 2nd December 1988, Mr Clarke[20] defined anonymous screening for HIV infection as involving the use of blood which had been taken voluntarily for other purposes but without specific consent for an HIV test. Before any test for HIV, all identifying details are to be removed from the sample to render the test wholly anonymous. The Government saw no legal obstacle to such testing or, from the layman's point of view, no ethical objections to the testing for scientific purposes of blood taken originally and properly for another purpose from a patient who was no longer identifiable. The Government therefore invited the Medical Research Council to submit proposals for a programme of anonymous testing. The Government later emphasised that the purpose of the testing was to obtain prevalence information and that it was important that people should not opt out[21].

The proposals submitted by the Medical Research Council about testing for HIV were wide ranging and covered both named and anonymous testing of many groups including ante-natal women. They repeat the Department of Health advice that there is no need to inform a patient that any residue of a blood sample taken for another purpose might be tested anonymously for HIV antibodies, and state that they expect that this information will not be given to patients involved in the projects. However, they also state that any patient who is aware that the testing is being carried out can request that his or her sample is not tested in this way and that this request must be respected.

A meeting in London in May 1989 to discuss the legal and ethical implications of these proposals was attended by many bodies with an interest in the matter of anonymous testing. The Department of Health and the three defence organisations stated that there seemed to be no legal obstacle provided that the blood sample had been obtained for a legitimate clinical purpose and that there had been appropriate consent for this. The General Medical Council and British Medical Association representatives expressed the opinion that they could see no legal or ethical objections but they also believed that the public ought to be made aware that there were studies being carried out in order to retain public trust in the medical profession. However, representatives of the Royal College of Nursing, Royal College of Midwives and Association of Health Visitors indicated that they believed that there were serious ethical objections to the anonymous testing of antenatal patients[22]. This was also the view taken by the House of Commons Social Services Committee which produced the first report on problems associated with AIDS in 1987. The committee takes the view that anonymised unlinked testing is unethical[23].

In November 1989, the Department of Health announced its plans for the extensive testing for HIV of unlinked anonymysed blood samples taken from patients in England and Wales. In a review of the scientific, legal and ethical basis for the research programme[24], it was stated that the MRC and BMA considered unlinked anonymous HIV testing to be ethically justifiable. It also stated that, after intensive examination of the proposals, the United Kingdom Central Council for Nursing, Midwifery and Health Visiting and the Royal College of Midwives have supported the current plans. This support is subject to the acceptance that members of the public must be made aware, whenever they have a blood sample taken, that any blood left over may be used anonymously for testing for HIV infection.

CONCLUSIONS

It is clear that, not only on legal and ethical grounds but also as a matter of good clinical practice, individual patients should only be tested for HIV infection after they have been properly and specifically counselled and with their informed consent. Patients whose tests are positive must be re-counselled. These conclusions apply to all specialities. In the particular case of obstetrics, the doctor must be informed and up to date so that appropriate advice can be given about whether an HIV positive patient should start or continue with a pregnancy, about the likely effect of the pregnancy on the progress of the infection or about the possibility of the fetus becoming infected.

Anonymised unlinked testing of pregnant women to measure the prevalence of HIV infection is a different matter. The scientific basis of the argument for anonymous unlinked testing is that uncertainties about an AIDS epidemic make it imperative that future monitoring surveys be sufficiently large, sustained and unbiased to provide valid estimates of the rate of change of infection in certain subgroups of the population. Anonymous unlinked screening can provide such unbiased results. Its implementation represents an important and necessary step forward towards improving our knowledge of the evolving HIV epidemic in this country. Provided anonymous unlinked testing of the target population runs in parallel with the usual named testing of individual patients who are counselled before and after testing, then the arguments that anonymous testing might harm individual patients cannot seriously be sustained. It seems that there are no major legal or ethical objections to it provided that it is truly anonymous and there is no way of connecting the sample being tested with an individual patient.

The entire population is likely to benefit from studies of this kind.

REFERENCES

1. Acquired Immune Deficiency Syndrome AIDS Booklet 3. DHSS, April 1986
2. Advisory Committee on Dangerous Pathogens; LAV/HTLV III—the causative agent of AIDS and related conditions. Revised guidelines. June 1986
3. Kennedy, I and Grubb A; Testing for HIV infection: the legal framework. The Law Society's Gazette (1989), No. 7, 15 Feb, 30–35
4. HIV testing: BMA consensus reached. British Medical Journal (1988), 297, 161–162
5. Confidentiality for doctors who are HIV positive. Lancet (1987), Nov. 21, 1221–1222
6. Doctors with AIDS and the 'News of the World'. British Medical Journal (1987), 295, 1339–1340
7. Royal College of Obstetricians and Gynaecologists; Report of the RCOG sub-committee on problems associated with AIDS in relation to obstetrics and gynaecology. Oct. 1987
8. AIDS and obstetrics and gynaecology; Proceedings of the Nineteenth Study Group of the Royal College of Obstetricians and Gynaecologists. March 1988
9. Bradbeer, Caroline; AIDS and family planning. British Journal of Family Planning (1988), 13, 25–27
10. Bury Judith K; Counselling women with HIV infection about pregnancy, heterosexual transmission and contraception. British Journal of Family Planning (1989), 14, 116–122
11. Re F (In Utero) [1988]; 2AII ER, 193
12. McKay v Essex Area Health Authority [1982]; 2WLR, 890
13. Norrie K McK, Lecturer in Law, University of Aberdeen. Private communication, 1989
14. McLean S, Director of Institute of Law and Ethics in Medicine, University of Glasgow, Private communication, 1989
15. Black D, Bodmer W, Cox D, Doll R et al; HIV testing on all pregnant women. Lancet, 1987, Nov 28, 1277
16. Smith J W G; Report of a working group on the monitoring and surveillance of HIV infection and AIDS, DHSS, May 1988
17. Testing for HIV infection. Lancet, 1988, June 4, 1293
18. Gold v Haringey Health Authority [1987], 3WLR, 649
19. Cox Report; Short-term prediction of HIV infection and AIDS. HMSO, 1988
20. Hansard, 2 December 1988, Written Answers, 440
21. Hansard, 13 January 1989. House of Commons Debate on AIDS, 1122
22. Simpson I G, Secretary, Joint Coordinating Committee, Medical defence organisations. Private communication, 1989
23. House of Commons, Social Services Committee, 7th Report, 1989, 8–9
24. Gill O N, Adler M W and Day N E; Monitoring the prevalence of HIV, British Medical Journal (1989) 299, 1295–8

14. Some legal implications of HIV/AIDS

S. A. M. McLean

As of this writing, it has been estimated that worldwide over 250 000 people have or have had AIDS (acquired immunodeficiency syndrome) and 5 to 10 million people may be affected with HIV (human immunodeficiency virus), the virus that is known to be linked to AIDS[1].

Disease, particularly contagious or infectious disease, has long fascinated society and confronted it with major dilemmas in balancing the values to be given to the freedom of individuals and the interests of society as a whole. As Wacks[2] has said: '[m]any medico-legal dilemmas frequently turn out to involve the conflict between autonomy and paternalism'[3]. Arguably, however, few, if any, diseases have generated such interest as has HIV infection or the syndrome to which it may lead, AIDS. As Wacks also said: '... the problems generated by the disease raise a plethora of profound moral and legal questions that cry out for urgent deliberation'.[4]

Because of the extent of the interest in these conditions, the public and the media have become involved in the discussion of its treatment and the treatment of sufferers in a way which is almost certainly unique. Moreover, the simplistic tendency to talk of 'high risk groups' rather than 'high risk practices' has provided fuel for those who wish to concentrate on the characteristics of those who most commonly (for the moment) suffer from these conditions, and has permitted discriminatory proposals or intervention to take place. These groups are most notably homosexual and bisexual men and intravenous drug users. Writing in 1990, Illingworth[5] says: 'Since 1981, when reporting began in the US, 63% of people with AIDS have either been homosexual or bisexual men, 7% homosexual or bisexual men with a history of IV drug-use, and 19% IV drug-users, both male and female'[6].

Evidence of this sort has apparently served to provoke prejudice, yet the heterosexual community can ill afford to be complacent. The evidence would now seem to suggest that no longer can the community make assumptions about those who are 'at risk', but rather that we should take seriously the question of 'high risk' practices. Harris, for example, notes that 'in the USA, 30% of those with AIDS are now heterosexual ...'[7]. Such information, whilst of concern to society, should nonetheless serve to minimise the discriminatory attitudes which have all too often been adopted. Indeed, the homosexual community has been widely respected for taking control of the problem and apparently beginning to contain it. The important message to come from this is that homosexuality is not the risk, but certain practices are. If this can be taken on board then many perceived legal problems, and much of the need for legal intervention, may in fact disappear. Restrictions relating, for example, to sexual orientation no longer make sense once the evidence is sensibly reviewed.

This point is important, since an appropriate and useful legal response will only be forthcoming if facts, rather than speculation or prejudice, are addressed. Viewing these conditions without filtering them through a screen of prejudice may permit us not to over-react. It should be borne in mind when considering those who are sufferers that, although there are regulations regarding the transmission of certain other transmissible diseases, and their reporting may be mandatory, there has been to date no policy of punishing those who suffer from them. Any regulations specifically designed to deal with this particular condition would therefore require—even historically—to be tested against the same standards, that is, against a background of respect for persons, anti-discrimination laws and the genuine interests of the community.

It should also be borne in mind that, to date at least, the transmission of the HIV virus is infinitely less predictable than the transmission, say, of tuberculosis. Individuals can, uniquely, assist in controlling both their capacity to transmit, and their vulnerability to contracting the virus. In any event, as Harris says: 'HIV is not easily passed from one person to another: it is a blood-borne virus, and is spread in fluids like semen, vaginal fluids, and blood'[8]. Arguably, the relative difficulty of spreading the condition, coupled with the capacity to control its spread by behavioural change, mean that less draconian measures may be needed with this condition than with others whose transmission seems to be arbitrary. Yet the calls for, and the reality of, legal intervention in respect of those who are vulnerable or suffering remain both strident and intense.

This chapter will look at a few of the legal problems that have already arisen in respect of those who seem to be vulnerable or who are infected with the HIV virus, and explore the ramifications of intervention, proposed or actual, in their lives. Concentration on one or two issues is essential, since the range of legal interest is enormous. It is not intended, therefore, to go into much detail about the entire spectrum of specific issues. Some of these will in any event have been considered in another chapter[9]. The purpose of this chapter is to concentrate on pointing to the genuine, and often unreasonable, prejudice and restrictions faced by those who are, after all, ill—not guilty.

If we look first at the rights of the individual, as guaranteed by international agreement, we can judge the extent to which these may be limited or removed in the case of the person who suffers from HIV/AIDS. Article 8 of the European Convention on Human Rights guarantees the following:

'Everyone has the right to respect for his private and family life, his home and his correspondence'. This would seem to suggest that an invasion of the privacy of individuals, say by compulsory testing for the virus, would be unacceptable. Yet, in 1987, the British Medical Association endorsed a policy of random screening for the virus, although in May 1988, they reversed this policy. Arguably, the recent announcement that random screening is to be carried out in certain sections of the community is an invasion of individual privacy, even if the results are to be anonymous[10].

The questions posed are, to what extent is such an invasion necessary or justified—indeed, is it an invasion? The BMA's reversal of their policy followed legal advice that positive HIV results carried a 'unique stigma'. Arguably this stigma is removed if the results are not made known to the patient. On the other hand, does not the doctor have a professional and moral commitment to ensure the safety of his/her patients—perhaps even of their partners? If so, can a failure to identify the victim not amount to some kind of professional incompetence or even negligence[11]?

To some extent, the question of whether or not random screening is an invasion of the rights of the individual as guaranteed by Article 8, is only answerable by reference to the exceptions to the general statement. As is the case with many international agreements, the general statement of a right is followed swiftly by a list of exceptions which may ultimately—although only on justification—water down the original right. In the case of Article 8, the relevant exception is as follows: (e) 'There shall be no interference by a public authority with the exercise of this right except as is in accordance with the law and is necessary in a democratic society in the interests of . . . public safety . . . for the protection of health or morals, or for the protection of the rights and freedoms of others.' The question to be answered, therefore, would seem to be is the risk of the transmission of the HIV virus proportionate to the interference with rights which random testing might entail? The answer is arguably less than clear. Let us take each part of the exception and consider its relevance to HIV/AIDS. The protection of public morals, mentioned in the exception, might be said by some— especially those who concentrate on the existence of high risk groups—to be sufficient reason to screen, for example, the homosexual community, who, to date, still represent the majority of those infected. Yet, is homosexuality a question of morality? In communities, such as the United Kingdom, where it is legalised between consenting adults in private, can we really continue to argue that sexual orientation is immoral? In some jurisdictions, of course, this argument continues to be used, although its value is un- certain. For example, Michael[12] points to cases in Eire and Northern Ireland which have been held to violate the right to privacy, by making homosexuality a criminal offence[13].

Moreover, if another part of the exception 'for the protection of health' is to be used as a valid reason for random, and unconsented to, screening, then we must surely know that such screening will *in fact* protect health. If the results are merely to be statistically collated, and are not to be used to identify carriers and to give them the opportunity to change their lifestyle in order to minimise the risk to others, in what sense can this be argued to be for the protection of health? Indeed, it is arguable that, although the terms seem to satisfy the letter of the European Convention, the Public Health (Infectious Diseases) Regulations 1985 breach the spirit of the Convention. These regulations give magistrates the power to detain an AIDS sufferer in hospital if he/she, on leaving hospital, does not have accommodation which provides proper precautions to prevent the spread of the disease. Is detention in a hospital, on such discretionary grounds, genuinely justified in the interests of the public's health?

Finally, the exception includes the capacity to limit the right where it is 'for the protection of the rights and freedoms of others'. Again, this is subject to the rule of proportionality, and it is not clear that the 'rights and freedoms of others' will be in any significant way enhanced by random testing, especially where such testing is anonymous and for statistical purposes only.

Yet many states have introduced regulations specifically designed to limit the freedoms of those who are thought to be at risk, who are HIV antibody positive, or who are known to be suffering from AIDS. Read in conjunction with Article 5 of the European Convention on Human Rights, and the Universal Declaration of Human Rights[14], it is not clear that these regulations can be justified. Article 5, for example, states that: 'Everyone has the right to liberty and security of person', implying, in conjunction with Article 8 of the European Convention, and Articles 3, 12 and 13 of the Universal Declaration[15] freedom of movement and freedom from intervention. Nonetheless, press reports in 1988[16] were able to list some 28 countries which have imposed some kind of requirements regarding HIV infection in respect of those thought likely to be at risk, or of all immigrants. In February 1988, for example, the South African Government announced that it was to deport 1000 black migrant workers who were HIV positive. In January 1989, it was announced that all Russians leaving the country for more than one month are to be tested for the virus on their return. And in August 1989, it was reported that a White Paper to be presented to the Australian Parliament proposed the compulsory testing of immigrants and refugees[17]. It was reported that migrants who tested positive would not automatically be excluded, but would be 'assessed on economic, compassionate and other grounds'[18].

Whilst the legitimate interests of any community might well be served by minimising the spread of this condition, it remains the case that measures of this sort are at best, relatively ineffective and, at worst, actually or potentially discriminatory. Indeed, '*The Times*' noted that migrant groups, although reluctant to criticise the White Paper until its terms were fully known, also cautioned that although 'the new proposals could be workable' this would be the case 'only if they are applied to migrants of all racial backgrounds wishing to enter Australia'[19].

Yet, despite the extent of restrictions currently imposed, their validity in the international context is at best dubious. As Shrimpton[20] notes:

It is at least doubtful whether international law and the International Health
Regulations in particular permit countries to discriminate against people with
AIDS, for example, by compulsorily testing passengers for HIV antibodies on
arrival. Most assuredly, the World Health Organization has not supported any
such moves and there is little expert support for them[21].

Quite apart from the problems confronting the would-be traveller or
immigrant, there are also immediate and direct difficulties confronting
those who are infected or who are under suspicion of being vulnerable.
Most significantly, these relate to employment opportunities and to the
availability of insurance policies and mortgages.

The history of discriminatory practices in employment and educational
opportunity is long—most commonly, its victims were chosen on the basis
of gender or colour. Despite legislation, it seems clear that such practices
have not altogether disappeared, but at least a framework for complaint
exists. HIV and AIDS provide yet another, and infinitely more complex
basis on which to discriminate. More complex because the discrimination
can be much more subtle—victims may not have any outward characteristics to which they themselves can refer in alleging discrimination, thereby
making proof of discrimination infinitely more difficult. The similarities,
however, are that all members of a group are likely victims, merely because
of their membership of the group—that is, independently of their own
habits or attitudes. All are therefore devalued or discriminated against[22].

The furore aroused by HIV infection and AIDS has been such that gay
men are perhaps uniquely vulnerable to discrimination, whatever their
practices and whatever their HIV antibody status. As Harris says: '... there
is an increasing amount of discrimination and prejudice towards people
with HIV or AIDS, or those believed to be infected or infectious. This
prejudice remains unchecked by the existing remedies of unfair dismissal.
Indeed, no present law affords employment protection to people affected by
AIDS'[23]. Yet, although there is no absolutely clear law tackling the HIV
carrier or the AIDS sufferer, it seems likely that a certain amount of
protection may be afforded to them via other anti-discrimination legislation. This, of course, is only the case where their victimisation is not
purely on real or suspected HIV status. Discrimination or differential
treatment on the grounds of actual ill-health or disability as a consequence
of any condition is likely to be covered by existing legislation. What is clear,
however, is that unstated and untested prejudice, which may well be a
catalyst for employment decisions, is less susceptible of external scrutiny
and less easily redressable.

There are, of course, some situations where the existence of AIDS or a
related condition is extremely relevant to employment. Thus, in 1987 the
President of the General Medical Council indicated that doctors who
believe themselves to be infected should seek specialist advice. This

recommendation was not designed to ensure or predict immediate dismissal, but rather was based on the fact that in some cases dementia may accompany the development of the condition, making them a risk to patients. What is problematic, however, is the situation where the possibility or the fact of infection is used as an excuse to terminate or refuse employment. In the United Kingdom, a homosexual, allegedly sacked because his fellow workers were afraid of catching AIDS from him, was awarded £2000 in an out-of-court settlement—small recompense for the loss of a job[24].

The rationale for discriminatory employment practices is less than clear. In almost every work situation—if not all of them—there would seem to be no real risk of transmission of the HIV virus. It cannot be contracted by sharing cups or toilets, and does not survive well once outside the body. Yet, fear of infection has undoubtedly informed and coloured the judgements of employers and co-workers. The issue was raised at a Governmental and judicial level in the United States in 1986/87.

In 1986, it was reported[25] that the US Justice Department had agreed that employers who believe that they are taking action to prevent the spread of AIDS may discriminate against people afflicted with the condition. Although civil rights laws do offer some protection to sufferers, it was felt that—unless the dismissal was a pretext for discrimination—it was not unlawful if the employer believed that the sufferer could spread the disease. The background to the case was that the US Department of Health and Human Services office of civil rights had received a number of complaints from hospital and clinic workers alleging that they had been discriminated against.

Discrimination based on handicap is expressly prohibited in any federally-funded or assisted programme by s.504 of the Rehabilitation Act 1973, and the question was whether or not this section applied in these circumstances. The Justice Department concluded that s.504 would prohibit discrimination based on the disabling effects of AIDS and related conditions, but that an individual's real or perceived ability to pass on the disease is not a handicap within the meaning of the statute, and accordingly that s.504 did not apply.

However, in 1987, the Supreme Court of the United States declined to rule on whether or not HIV infection was a handicap within the meaning of the Act. They did, however, seem to countenance the possibility that irrational prejudicial behaviour would be condemned, saying:

Society's accumulated myths and fears about disability and disease are as handicapping as are the physical limitations that flow from actual impairment. Few aspects give rise to the same level of public fear and misapprehension as contagiousness . . . The Act [1973 Rehabilitation Act] is carefully structured to replace such reflexive reactions to actual or perceived handicaps with actions based on reasoned and medically sound judgments[26].

Just as discrimination in employment is a characteristic of the treatment of those thought or known to be at risk or infected, so too is discrimination in the provision of insurance cover or mortgage facilities. Failure to obtain either of these may dramatically affect the well-being of sufferers and their families. Equally, suspicion of vulnerability—again by concentrating on groups rather than practices—may lead to the non-infected and those not at risk being denied these facilities also. There are two distinct problems here. One relates to those who are infected and the other to those who are thought to be vulnerable to infection.

In 1988, the Institute of Actuaries called upon the insurers who offer permanent health insurance to exclude AIDS and AIDS related conditions from cover. The rationale for this is, of course, financial, but it is equally the case that such considerations may cause unwarranted suffering. However, even if one can accept this type of exclusion, the extent of the prejudice can be seen from the way in which prospective customers may be dealt with if they are thought to be in a 'high risk group'. Not only has it been widely acknowledged that those who test HIV antibody positive will be unlikely to receive cover, but even those who have a negative test may find their capacity to obtain cover limited or removed. The mere fact of having the test has been used by some companies as evidence that the person is in a 'high risk group' and insurance is therefore declined, or premiums heavily loaded. As Gryk[27] says:

It is ... unfortunate that the lack of an insurance regulatory structure in the UK has made it impossible to ensure that the very many public policy issues arising in this area are addressed. This has meant that many of the approaches taken thus far by the industry have been unduly self-serving and discriminatory, and largely based on surmise rather than fact. In particular, the insurance industry has failed to acknowledge that those at risk of HIV infection cannot be simplistically identified by seeking to establish the membership of individuals to particular limited groups[28].

The concern about denial of insurance and/or mortgage cover has been considerable. The British Medical Association, not surprisingly concerned about the possible implications of disclosure of HIV antibody status, has indicated that 'campaigns to prevent the spread of AIDS will be jeopardised if people are denied life insurance simply because they have previously undergone an AIDS test ...'[29]. Yet, it was reported on the same day that 'people with negative tests for AIDS are being denied life assurance, despite the big insurance companies saying that no one should be debarred from cover merely because they have been tested ...'[30]. On February 11, 1989 the Association of British Insurers issued a leaflet stating that 'having an AIDS blood test is no bar to getting life insurance ...'. As they said 'anyone who has had an HIV (AIDS) blood test, the result of which is negative, should be able to get the life cover they want unless there are other circumstances affecting the particular risk'[31]. However, so intense has the problem been that it was reported on June 24 1989 that 'a Commons select committee is to urge the Government to stop insurance companies increasing premiums for clients who have AIDS tests'[32].

Yet the truth is that lifestyle questionnaires, based on 'risk groups' rather than 'risk practices' remain central to the provision of insurance cover. One wonders, also, what will be the implications of compulsory HIV testing. Ultimately, to be a genuine contribution to patient care, these tests will have to be attributable—that is, there is only so long that they can humanely or realistically be used only for statistical purposes. The insurance industry, amongst others, will have to consider the possible implications of a scheme of compulsory testing on those who test negative or positive, and the medical profession will have to consider the question of confidentiality. Moreover, as their own professional association has pointed out, doctors will have to be wary of speculating about lifestyle, since it would seem that there may be a risk that some patients may be denied cover because of 'impressions gained by doctors' rather than from any scientifically testable evidence[33].

The problem of what to do in respect of those who are infected or who are at risk will not go away and is not easily resolved. It was reported in the press on June 30 1989 that the 'world's first insurance policy against catching AIDS was launched yesterday in Britain'[34]. The policy, according to a different press report was aimed at 'those in "high risk" professions such as doctors, nurses, ambulance staff and other emergency services ...', and was denounced by the Terrence Higgins Trust and the British Medical Association[35]. The scheme, launched by Lloyd's underwriters and an AIDS charity, Lifeshield Foundation, apparently does not yet cover gay people and drug users, although the proposers say that they hope it will ultimately do so. According to the 'Financial Times' 'no medical evidence is required at the outset, but individuals must declare that they are not HIV positive at the start of the contract; do not inject drugs other than those prescribed by a doctor: do not indulge in non-heterosexual activities; and will not deliberately inflict the HIV virus'[36]. On the other hand, only a few days later Laurentian Life, described by 'The Guardian' as one of the leading British underwriting groups, said that 'victims of the HIV virus ... are uninsurable ...'[37].

Certainly, the impact of paying attention to so-called 'high risk groups' cannot be underestimated. In November 1989, it was reported that, as a result of insurance companies' fears about HIV/AIDS, 'the cost of the most common types of life assurance, essential to most mortgages, has doubled in some areas ...'[38]. For the sufferer, however, one possible breakthrough has recently been announced. In January 1990, the Prudential Insurance Company of America announced what may be a breakthrough of sorts for those currently dying of diseases such as AIDS[39]. The company announced its Living Needs Benefit Programme, which would pay out a lump sum of monthly repayments to those who can provide evidence that they have six months or less to live. This could clearly provide much needed assistance for those for whom the cost of terminal care is prohibitive, for example the person dying of cancer or AIDS. And, whatever any potential drawbacks may be, such a scheme at least has the merit of addressing itself to *real* sufferers rather than those who only might be at risk.

CONCLUSIONS

Without being comprehensive in its coverage of potential legal problems, this chapter has argued that concentration on membership of a group rather than on practices which facilitate the contraction and spread of the HIV virus has permitted—indeed facilitated—discrimination and prejudice.

It is often the case that legal intervention is neither necessary nor appropriate in the resolution of social or medical problems, and certainly it is clear that the law cannot solve the problems of HIV/AIDS. However, even this brief look at some of the issues shows that some actual or potential sufferers may be penalised or have their rights and liberties infringed. This seems to suggest that there is in this case a role which the law can usefully play in minimising discrimination. This role is not one, therefore, which reinforces stereotypes or imposes harsh conditions, but rather one which reinforces respect for persons and anti-discrimination principles, by providing a relevant framework both to prevent infringement of rights or to provide remedial measures where infringement does take place. In this respect the law plays its traditional role of balancing and respecting rights and freedoms.

NOTES

1. Illingworth P, AIDS and the Good Society, London, Routledge, 1990, at p. 1
2. Wacks R, 'Controlling AIDS—Some Legal Issues', 138 New Law Journal 254 (1988)
3. at p. 254
4. id.
5. op. cit.
6. at p. 1
7. Harris D, 'AIDS, people with AIDS, and Legal Advice, in Harris D and Haigh R (eds), AIDS: A Guide to the Law, London, Routledge, 1990 (book produced for the Terrence Higgins Trust), at p. 2
8. loc. cit., at p. 2
9. see Watson J in this book
10. see chapter 13, infra
11. For example, if the doctor treats both a sufferer and his/her sexual partner, then that doctor owes a duty of care to both of them. This duty encapsulates a duty not to omit to do something (e.g. not to omit to warn of risks) as well as a duty to act positively for the patient's benefit
12. Michael J, 'Homosexuals and Privacy', 183 New Law Journal 831 (1988)
13. In the cases of Dudgeon (Northern Ireland—1981) and Norris (Eire—1988)
14. Adopted on 10 December 1948. Article 1 says: 'All human beings are born free and equal in dignity and rights. They are endowed with reason and conscience and should act towards one another in a spirit of brotherhood.' Article 2: 'Everyone is entitled to all the rights and freedoms set forth in this Declaration, without distinction of any kind, such as race, colour, sex, language, religion, political or other opinion, national or social origin,

property, birth or other status.' Article 3: 'Everyone has the right to life, liberty and security of person.'

15. Article 12: 'No one shall be subjected to arbitrary interference with his privacy, family, home or correspondence, nor to attacks upon his honour and reputation. Everyone has the right to the protection of the law against such interference or attacks.' Article 13: '1) Everyone has the right to freedom of movement and residence within the borders of each state. 2) Everyone has the right to leave any country, including his own, and to return to his country.'
16. cf. 'The Guardian' 11 May 1988
17. cf. 'The Times' 29 August 1989
18. 'The Daily Telegraph' 29 August 1989
19. 'The Times' 29 August 1989
20. Shrimpton M, 'AIDS and immigration' in Harris and Haigh, op. cit.
21. at p. 111
22. For a discussion of the nature of discrimination, see Campbell T D, 'Sex Discrimination: Mistaking the Relevance of Gender', in McLean, S A M and Burrows N (eds), The Legal relevance of Gender: Some Aspects of Sex Based Discrimination, London, The Macmillan Press, 1988
23. Harris D, 'AIDS and employment' in Harris and Haigh, op. cit.
24. For discussion of this case and others, see Harris D, 'AIDS and employment', supra cit. note 23
25. Santa Barbara News-Press, 23 June 1986
26. School Board of Nassau County v Arline 107 S. Ct. 1123 (1987)
27. Gryk W, 'AIDS and insurance' in Harris and Haigh, op. cit.
28. at p. 142
29. 'The Guardian' 6 February 1989
30. 'The Independent' 6 February 1989
31. 'The Times' 11 February 1989
32. 'The Times' 24 June 1989
33. 'The Times' 6 February 1989
34. 'The Guardian' 30 June 1989
35. cf. 'The Independent' 30 June 1989; 'The Times' 30 June 1989
36. 'Financial Times' 30 June 1989
37. 'The Guardian' 8 July 1989
38. 'The Independent' 4 November 1989
39. 'The Guardian' 29 January 1990

15. Ante-natal screening for HIV— review and case for anonymysed unlinked studies

F. D. Johnstone

INTRODUCTION

HIV testing of pregnant women is a subject which arouses strong feelings and has provoked fierce debate over the last few years. Much of this debate has arisen because of confusion between testing as part of clinical care, and screening of populations for surveillance purposes. In this paper I will review the test itself, the objections which have been raised to anonymysed unlinked testing and will argue that a combination of total anonymysed unlinked screening for surveillance, and HIV testing of the individual after informed consent, is the ethically correct and most practicable response at this stage in the development of the epidemic.

THE HIV TEST

Routinely used tests do not measure the virus itself but antibodies to the virus. The antibody response associated with HIV infection is directed against a variety of viral proteins; gp 160, gp 120 and gp 41 encoded by the env gene; p 55, p 24, p 18 and p 15 encoded by the gag gene; and p 64, p 53 and p 31 encoded by the pol gene. Commercially available tests to different proteins use enzyme linked immunoadsorbent assay (ELISA), direct antibody capture radioimmunoassay or competitive radioimmunoassay and recently available test kits use recombinant viral antigens. Positive results are confirmed with a different test system against different viral proteins, and doubtful cases are checked with Western blotting. It is good practice, particularly when the result is unexpected, to confirm with another blood sample from the patient. Such a multistep algorithm was used by Burke et al (1988) in the first 20 months of testing a very low risk population (civilian applicants for US military service). This involved an ELISA test (1% false positive) a retest with a different ELISA, then if still positive Western blotting (with conservative criteria for interpretation) and finally retesting a further specimen with Western blotting. Under these conditions the false positive rate was 1 in 135 187 persons tested. However this was in the early days of testing and the authors believe the false positive rate is now substantially less because of improvements in their methodology.

Mortimer (1989) analysed different testing strategies and pointed out that if three truly independent assays were applied, each 99% specific, the false positivity rate would be one per million. The proportion of positive tests which are false positives will therefore be greater where the prevalence of HIV in the population is extremely low. Using Baye's theorem, Lo et al (1989) calculated that the positive predictive value in female first time blood donors with no risk factors could be as low as 0.65. Interpretation errors can occur with reactivity to non-viral proteins on Western blot and Healy and Howard (1989) emphasise conservative minimum criteria for diagnosis; they require typical reactivity to one or more glycoproteins and at least three other viral specific bands. Not all laboratories have such a strict protocol. Quality control showed that 10 of 19 laboratories failed proficiency testing at least once (CDC 1988). New techniques should mean improved sensitivity and specificity and the main risk is human error. With constant vigilance, and providing the laboratory employs strict criteria such as those described above, the chance of a definite and repeatedly false positive result in an adult is remote.

On the other hand, false negative results do occur because of the delay between infection and the appearance of antibody. Although this is usually less than three months (generally 3–12 weeks) there is evidence from DNA amplification studies, using polymerase chain reaction (Ou et al, 1988) suggesting that the delay can be up to 36 months (Imagawa et al, 1989, Pezzella et al, 1989) confirming earlier suspicions (Ranki et al, 1987). Though this does seem to be a real phenomenon, it is probably not common. Horsburgh et al (1989) estimate that it occurs in less than 5% of infected individuals. Nevertheless testing in high risk individuals should be repeated until at least one year after the last risk exposure.

CONSENT TO ATTRIBUTABLE TESTING

Where the result of a test is attributable, that is the patient is identified, there is a clear ethical obligation to obtain fully informed consent. There is probably also a legal requirement. Sherrard and Gatt (1987) advised the British Medical Association's council that if doctors tested for HIV without explicit consent, they could be laying themselves open to negligence actions or even criminal liability. A further legal opinion (also referred to by Dyer, 1988) disagreed with this. Mr Leo Charles QC told the Central Committee for Hospital Medical Services that it would be up to the doctor's clinical judgement whether to tell the patient the test was for HIV. Dickens (1988) has given a detailed account of legal issues and problems surrounding HIV testing in the US, and Orr (1989) considered the implications of HIV for British and American law.

Admittedly it is possible to construct theoretical examples of cases where testing without consent might be in the best interest of the patient, but such cases are exceptional, would need very careful consideration, and should not detract from the general principles of testing which have been well stated by Eickhof (1988). He cited five overriding principles that must be addressed;

The policy must support a defined goal for the health of the patient, her contacts or the public health. The patient must be informed and testing consented to by the patient. Testing must always be accompanied by counselling and guidance. Health and hospital care must not be in any way conditional on consenting to be tested or the results of the test. The confidentiality of test results must be maintained.

How vigorously attributable testing should be advocated has also been discussed. Weiss and Thier (1988) urge caution and being very clear about the reasons for testing any individual, whereas Rhame and Maki (1989) claim that testing should be strongly recommended, by stressing the advantages, to all adults under the age of 60 in the United States. Opinion on this issue is likely to change as the epidemic changes, and particularly, as more effective treatment is developed. The benefits and harms of voluntary screening have been excellently reviewed by Lo et al (1989).

Although mandatory testing has been advocated, perhaps as a require-ment before acceptance for ante-natal and delivery care, this appears a serious infringement of human rights. In addition, from a practical point of view there are major disadvantages such as alienation of individuals from health care, with few major benefits as far as controlling the epidemic is concerned. The historical perspective of other sexually transmitted diseases (Brandt 1988) and the epidemic so far (Kirby 1988) teaches us that coercive policies are unsuccessful and there is a broad consensus among those clinically involved against any mandatory testing in the health care setting.

How much counselling is required before testing? This depends to a certain extent on assessment of risk. If a woman is at high risk (shared needles, or has a seropositive sexual partner) then very detailed information about the test and the implications of a positive and negative result for her and the pregnancy is necessary. Women who have carefully considered whether to take the test and have been aware of all the implications are much better prepared if the result turns out to be positive, and careful pretest counselling may mitigate some of the negative effects (James 1988, Glover and Miller 1989). Sherer (1988) gives an impressive account of the potential pitfalls of testing and the importance of detailed counselling, and he advises 'consent, counselling, confidentiality and caution'. Pre and post test counselling is discussed in a general way by Glover and Miller (1989) and in the pre-natal care setting by Holman et al (1989a and 1989b).

Where the pregnant woman is at very low risk, then there has to be a balance between the advantages and disadvantages of counselling (see below), and a shorter general explanation of the test without going into all the detailed implications of a positive result seems appropriate.

ADVANTAGES AND DISADVANTAGES OF TESTING TO THE INDIVIDUAL

Advantages

HIV infection results in a relentlessly progressive destruction of the immune system and infection is lifelong. There is no cure. Early in the epidemic it seemed that there were few advantages to the individual in being tested but this position has now changed. Counselling and a negative test may reinforce behaviour patterns which decrease the chance of becoming infected, and may also relieve considerable anxiety. However, knowledge that she is seropositive also carries a number of advantages to the pregnant woman (Minkoff and Landesman 1988, Volberding 1989, Duff 1989). In the first place, in view of the 22–39 per cent probability of infecting her child (European Collaborative Study 1988, Italian Multi-centre Study 1988, Blanche et al 1989, Ryder et al 1989) she has the opportunity to consider termination of pregnancy, though in practice, this does not seem to be an option readily exercised by women with a wanted pregnancy (Selwyn et al 1989, Johnstone et al 1990).

There are also precautions which can be taken which may minimise the chance of infecting the baby (avoiding scalp electrodes and fetal blood sampling in labour, bottle rather than breast feeding). The infant can be monitored carefully and treated more readily for infections. The woman herself can be watched carefully for symptoms or signs of progression of disease, as such symptoms can be ascribed to pregnancy itself (Minkoff et al 1986). In the longer term she has an opportunity to develop a health promoting lifestyle, to start Zidovudine (AZT) at the appropriate time (Lancet 1989) to use prophylactic aerosolised pentamidine, and to benefit from the other partially effective treatments for HIV infection which will be developed. Finally she is enabled to take steps to protect her sexual partner(s) and make informed decisions about future childbearing.

Disadvantages

The psychological costs of screening in general have been discussed by Marteau (1989). A negative result, if the significance is poorly understood, could reinforce some women in a risk taking behaviour pattern, or maintain a pre-existing sense of invulnerability. There may also be great difficulties in coping with a positive test result (James 1988, Glover and Miller 1989). The added burden of knowledge of being infected may be too much for women already under great pressure from social, relationship or psychological problems. This may result in excessive drug taking activity. Suicide rates are far higher in individuals with AIDS and there are suggestions that death from overdose may be more common in HIV seropositive than HIV seronegative drug users (Johnstone unpublished data).

Even having had a test may under certain circumstances cause discrimination in the hospital setting. In many hospitals women who are found to be seropositive, or who declare a high risk activity, have restricted access to a number of laboratory tests and are treated differently clinically. The degree of difference varies from slight modifications in staff clothing and disposal of blood and other body fluids, which do not affect care and will not be noticed by the patient, through to clearly discriminatory procedures which can have a major effect on the patient's experience in hospital, and may be noticed by visitors. This should not happen, but can do so where there is not an upgraded one tier system of infection control.

In theory the test result is entirely confidential, and test information is shared only with those who 'need to know'. However, in the maternity hospital setting this includes a very large number of people, and there are concerns that confidentiality could break down in some cases. There are many examples of discrimination against individuals who are known to be seropositive. Physical violence and damage to property, sexual or social isolation within the individual's community are real fears. In the United States there have been examples of loss of jobs, housing, and restriction of travel; a positive test bars entry to the military, Peace Corps and several other government positions. Laws proposing severe curtailment of civil liberties have been put forward in several different parts of the world. Insurance companies are very reluctant to insure HIV infected women and it may be impossible to get a mortgage. Blendon and Donelan (1988) review more than 50 national and international opinion surveys and conclude that it is not possible to reassure those testing seropositive that they will be protected from potentially discriminatory consequences. Between 1 in 4 and 1 in 5 people in the US believed that those with 'AIDS' should be excluded from working with them, attending school with their children and living in their neighbourhood. Without consideration of the logistics, 30% expressed support for 'quarantining' the more than 1 million people estimated to be infected with HIV in the United States.

ADVANTAGES FOR THE PUBLIC HEALTH

There are two possible advantages from testing or screening as far as Public Health is concerned. The first is that with counselling and testing of the individual there may be modification of lifestyle which may decrease spread of disease; the second is that population prevalence studies will provide essential data about development of the epidemic.

Behaviour modification

Does providing counselling and testing modify behaviour in a beneficial direction? Cates and Handsfield (1988) review the available information and conclude that the answer is probably yes, but that the change is of relatively small magnitude and not found in all studies.

Some studies in homosexual men have shown that knowledge of sero-positivity leads to a decrease in high risk sexual behaviour (Schechter et al 1988, Van Griensven et al 1988). In drug users, Des Jarlais et al (1987) reported that those who are seropositive decrease needle sharing, though with little change in sexual behaviour. There is no information about pregnant women. The overall belief, although with little substantial data, is that testing and counselling can provide some public health benefit by reducing the spread of HIV (CDC 1987, Francis and Chin 1987). However, the great complexity of behaviour and its modification, particularly in intimate aspects of women's lives, is emphasised in an excellent review by Becker and Joseph (1988).

Surveillance

The average time between infection and development of AIDS is thought to be about nine years and this is likely to become longer as treatment of asymptomatic individuals with AZT becomes more common (Lancet 1989). AIDS figures therefore reflect what was happening nearly 10 years ago, and do not tell us about the current situation. It is therefore essential to gather information on prevalence of HIV infection, geographical distribution and frequency in different risk groups. These data allow accurate mathematical modelling, and will allow planning of health care facilities. As the Social Services Committee (1987) concluded 'without knowledge of how the virus is spreading and calculations of the numbers that will have to be cared for, current plans for health services and education are based on nothing more than guess work'. The information should also help in determining screening policies at local level. In the UK and USA, the infection is still very patchily distributed and the health care response at different areas should also be different depending on prevalence and predicted clinical load.

CLINICAL TESTING PROGRAMMES

Selective testing

This involves case finding, by noting risk features from the history (Table 15.1) and offering selected patients counselling and testing if wanted. This is the method suggested as appropriate by the Royal College of Obstetricians and Gynaecologists (1987) and as carried out initially in Edinburgh (Johnstone et al 1989). It is cheap, and likely to be effective early in the course of the epidemic, when infection is limited to women with a clear risk factor. If this approach is used it is important that an individual can also have testing without declaring a risk activity.

As the epidemic progresses, this approach becomes less satisfactory. Women infected heterosexually may be unaware that they are at risk, women may not acknowledge to themselves they are at risk and there may

Table 15.1   High risk groups for selective HIV testing in pregnant women (taken from RCOG 1987)

a) Sexual partners of men who have had sex with other men at any time since 1977.
b) Drug users or sexual partners of drug users who have injected themselves with drugs at any time since 1977.
c) Women who have had sex at any time since 1977 with people living in African countries except those on the Mediterranean, or who have sexual partners who have done so.
d) Sexual partners of haemophiliacs.
e) Women who are prostitutes.

also be concealment of risk activities from health care staff. Thus, although in Paris a large study concluded that most individuals might have been identified by selective testing (Brossard et al 1988) this was not found to be the case in several studies in the United States. Quinn et al (1987) in a sexually transmitted disease clinic in Baltimore found that nearly half of infected women failed to acknowledge the presence of known risk factors for HIV acquisition. Landesman et al (1987) similarly found that 42% of seropositive pregnant women denied risk factors at a screening interview. Voluntary testing in other US antenatal clinics (compared with total anonymysed screening) detected only 4 of 28 seropositive women in one study (Kraskinski et al 1988) and 9 of 26 HIV positive women in another (Connor et al, 1988). Sperling et al (1989) detected none of 6 seropositive women in a voluntary programme based on self acknowledged risk behaviour. In one study in London, only 9 of 1500 ante-natal women were tested in a voluntary scheme based on selection by risk, but 12 of 2200 sera tested anonymously were positive (Heath et al 1988). In areas of high prevalence, selective testing seems to be an insufficient way of detecting HIV infected women. Each geographical area therefore needs to define its testing and screening programme in response to surveillance data.

Universal testing

Where there is an appreciable prevalence in the ante-natal community, there are strong arguments for offering all women an HIV test along with the other booking bloods. This has been argued in detail above and also by Minkoff and Landesmann (1988) and Duff (1989). Nevertheless there are negative aspects to this approach. It is expensive in counselling time and testing. It may arouse anxiety unnecessarily (Stevens et al 1989, Sherr et al 1989). Some women may feel coerced into being tested. Finally, discussion of HIV testing may overshadow the many other facets of ante-natal care discussed at the booking visit, and arguably could result in negative feelings towards the hospital staff.

SURVEILLANCE

It must be emphasised that pregnant women are only one of many groups who must be studied if accurate data on population prevalence are to be obtained. Pregnant women are however of considerable interest epidemiologically as they will give some guide to the extent of spread by heterosexual intercourse. This in the long term is what will determine the size of the epidemic in the UK.

I will argue that surveillance is best carried out by anonymysed unlinked screening in combination with voluntary attributable screening but I will discuss these methods separately.

Voluntary, attributable screening

This is the method of surveillance advocated by Howie (1988), and there is an ongoing study, funded by the MRC in Edinburgh and Dundee using this design. Compared with total anonymysed unlinked screening it has the epidemiological advantage that any seropositive cases can be further questioned to try to determine the source of infection, whether the woman was a covert drug user or was infected by heterosexual intercourse, for example. However, this study design has a major flaw. In many situations it does not give population prevalence data. Voluntary testing after counselling was accepted by only 74% of women in a study in New York (Holman et al 1989), 78% of women in Chicago (Barton et al 1989), 75% in Edinburgh (Reid, Scrimegeour, unpublished data) and 74% in London (Howard et al 1989). Much higher acceptance rates have been obtained in Norway, Sweden and Finland, where prevalence is extremely low (Brattebo and Wiseborg 1988) and also in Paris where prevalence is relatively high (Brossard et al 1988). There is one study from the US with a high rate of acceptance (Lindsay et al 1989). It is not clear why there are these differences, and whether the same counselling and opportunity to refuse exists in these other studies.

It might be expected that those refusing testing might have a higher prevalence of infection than those consenting, and there is ample evidence that this is indeed the case. Hull et al (1988) for example found that 82% of those attending a sexually transmitted disease clinic accepted testing, and their seroprevalence was 0.7%. Those refusing were tested anonymously (unlinked) and 3.8% were seropositive. More than 50% of infected persons therefore refused testing, and those refusing were more than five times more likely to be infected. Particularly where true prevalence in many areas of the UK (outside London and Scotland) may be 0.01% or lower (Gill et al 1989) it can be seen that attributable testing on its own will not provide accurate prevalence data. It is also expensive, mainly in counselling time.

Anonymysed (unlinked) screening

Residual blood taken for other tests during pregnancy, or Guthrie Cards from the baby (Hoff 1988) are used instead of being discarded (Gillett

1989). Before testing, there may be some information retained (e.g. geographical area, age or parity) and in some studies the bloods have been linked to a questionnaire about risk activity (Landesman et al 1987) but all other identifiers are removed so that there is no possibility of tracing a result back to an individual. This gives accurate prevalence data but there is no opportunity to question the individual to find out the infection source. It is cheap, involving little more than the cost of the test. The principles have been well described (Gill et al 1989).

This method is not new. Immunity prevalence to measles, poliomyelitis, rubella, diptheria and tetanus is already assessed by anonymysed screening. Levels of antibody to influenza virus are monitored to help determine the appropriate content to influenza vaccine each year. Anonymysed unlinked testing is extensively used in the United States to monitor prevalence of HIV in different sections of the population and in different geographical areas. No major logistic or ethical problems seem to have been encountered. Although most epidemiologists favour anonymysed unlinked screening as a useful way to establish prevalence and such testing has been strongly supported by the World Health Organization Global Programme on AIDS, there has been limited use of this method in the UK. This is largely because of the perceived problems which will now be discussed. A useful insight into the debate can be gained from the Social Services Committee 3rd Report Problems Associated with Aids (1987). In this the committee advised parliament against anonymysed screening mainly on the evidence given by Professor Ian Kennedy, Centre of Medical Law and Ethics, King's College, London. The case against anonymysed screening has also been argued, though much less vociferously, by Gillon (1987), Senior Fellow, Centre for Medical Law and Ethics, King's College, London, and by representatives of the Royal College of Obstetricians and Gynaecologists (Howie et al 1987, Howie 1988, Hudson et al 1988). However, it should be clear that these opinions were expressed up to three years ago, and may not represent these individuals' current view.

OBJECTIONS TO ANONYMYSED UNLINKED SCREENING

1. *The seropositive individual cannot be identified and informed of the result.* This is true by design, and is probably the central objection to this type of screening. Gillon (1987) puts it most strongly; this is 'one of the most morally offensive aspects of anonymous prevalence screening for HIV antibody'. In his evidence to the Social Services Committee (1987), MacDonald (1987), the Chief Medical Officer for Scotland pointed to this as the main ethical problem that 'if some tests came up positive there is then no way of going back to the patient'. An extension of this theme is the suggestion by Howie (1988) that health care workers would not be enabled to take suitable precautions to protect themselves against transmission of infection.

This argument shows a failure to understand the difference between clinical testing and surveillance screening. Screening is not an alternative to testing. It simply reports data where none would otherwise exist. Any woman who wants to have an identified test should have one, and in areas where seroprevalence is shown to be high, all women should be counselled and offered testing, as discussed above. The place of anonymysed screening is in establishing prevalence where testing is, for whatever reason, not being done. Bayer (1989) points to the irony that 'what few objections were made were not from those concerned about individual rights but from some public health officials and clinicians. It was precisely the features of blinded seroprevalence studies that recommended them to those concerned about privacy that such opponents found most disturbing'.

2. *If it's bad science, it's bad ethics.* Much has been made by the antagonists of anonymysed screening of the supposed scientific defects of such prevalence data. Despite the fact that the early proposal came from Sir Richard Doll (1987), at that time Chairman of the epidemiological sub-committee of the Medical Research Council's working party on AIDS, Kennedy (1987) in his evidence to the Social Services Committee, claimed that it was bad science, and that 'if it is bad scientifically, it's bad ethically'.

The first criticism is that the source of infection cannot be known. Howie (1988) stated that 'the quality of prevalence studies will be reduced when anonymous testing is used because it will be more difficult to identify high and low risk individuals with confidence', and again that anonymous testing would 'gravely limit the value from an epidemiological and scientific point of view' (Howie 1987). These opinions are not shared by many epidemiologists as will be discussed below. Of course women who declare high risk activities will in any system be offered testing separately but the point of population screening is simply to get prevalence data. If the prevalence is very low, as it is likely to be in most parts of the UK at present, then the mode of transmission for each individual case is less important.

The second criticism is that there would be so many false positive tests (without being able to check another sample from the individual) that anonymysed testing would give misleading results. Howie considered 'it is highly likely that pregnancy may produce a very large number of false positive results for HIV'. This criticism, as repeated by Hudson et al (1988), was considered to show 'a serious misunderstanding of the procedures used by the Regional Blood Transfusion Services and by the Public Health Laboratory Service' (Entwhistle & Selcon 1988). Techniques and experience have also increased considerably since that time and few virologists would agree that false positivity is now a major problem in such a study.

The Social Services Committee (1987) on the basis of the evidence they had heard, also criticised anonymous screening on statistical grounds. Two examples are quoted by Black et al (1987). Firstly, the report states: 'The total projected sample would be so huge as to render the information gained worthless'. As Black et al comment, this shows a worrying misunder-standing of elementary statistics. Also, as Glynn (1987) pointed out, well planned studies in a few strategically placed areas would give the required information. The report goes on to state that 'it would be more useful and accurate to seek to construct mathematical models by which the future spread of infection can be predicted using computers'. This also suggests a limited understanding, because data on prevalence are an accompaniment of mathematical modelling, not an alternative.

As has been emphasised above, screening pregnant women is only one aspect of population prevalence and gives limited information. The inability to know risk activity is a serious disadvantage. Pregnant women are not necessarily representative of all sexually active women. Performed on a large scale, such studies are expensive. Nevertheless pregnant women are thought to be an important group epidemiologically, and the comments above together with the decision of the Social Services Committee, were heavily criticised by a number of eminent individuals, most of whom had a statistical or epidemiological background (Black et al 1987). The epidemi-ological arguments for such testing have again recently been stated (Gill et al 1989).

3. *Such testing may contravene international guidelines on medical re-search.* Gillon (1987) quotes the World Medical Association's Declaration of Helsinki on the principles that should underline medical research on human subjects. This states that 'subjects should be volunteers' and that each potential subject must be 'adequately informed'. This argument is probably misleading because these statements, while they are unexcep-tional and almost axiomatic as regards any interventionist research, do not necessarily apply to the use of discarded blood. Lucas (1988) illustrated this by terming this 'audit' rather than research. He takes the example of Caesarean section statistics. If, for example, a researcher studied variations in Caesarean section around the country, no one would expect him to contact each patient to adequately inform them before drawing up his tables. Although this is a far-fetched example, it illustrates that the particular quotations Gillon chooses were not drawn up with this type of study in mind. The World Health Organization considers such testing to be 'consistent with existing guidelines on human rights in biomedical research' (WHO 1989).

4. *The patient's interests are violated if explicit consent is not given.* This is the basic principle underlying other ethical objections. Blood removed from a patient belongs to her, and she has a right to decide exactly what happens to that blood. This has been stated most emphatically by Kennedy (1987) in his evidence to the Social Services Committee. He thought there were 'grave ethical objections' to anonymysed screening without specific individual consent. He considered that 'the patient's interests are violated' and that it would result in 'undermining the doctor-patient relationship with the possibility of those most at risk going underground'. These

principles came from 'the heritage we have acquired from Nuremberg and afterwards'.

Gillon (1987) also considers the ethics of testing anonymously without specific consent. In a telling and very interesting section in his article, Gillon discusses why, although the individual may not be harmed, moral principles dictate that certain types of behaviour—and he takes the example of deceit—be avoided. He develops this theme and concludes that the particular trust a patient has in her doctor could break down if 'we trade on a deceit, and use that patient for the benefit of others'.

This is clearly a very important point, but does depend somewhat on the attitude of patients to 'discarded' blood. In the United States, where there has been extensive use of anonymysed testing, there do not appear to have been any objections to the collection of this information. Many would share the concept that testing discarded and unlabelled blood is like testing the drains (Thornton 1987) or that it is simply audit (Lucas 1988); that it is devoid of individual significance once the identifiers have been removed and it has been merged into a very large population.

As reviewed by Gill et al (1989) many organisations have accepted that no fundamental ethical principles are breached by anonymysed unlinked testing, including the British government, the Medical Defence Societies, the General Medical Council, the Medical Research Council, the Health Education Authority and the Royal College of Midwives. Secrecy is a separate issue. The data produced will only serve a function if accessible to researchers and public health workers. It must therefore be in the public domain after collection, and therefore the public should be fully informed beforehand. There is therefore the possibility of spontaneous refusal. A pregnant woman might refuse to have blood taken for other tests if the discarded blood was to be used for anonymysed HIV testing. In this case her essential medical care could not be dependent on participation in a surveillance study and she would have to be given a guarantee that her blood would not be so used. Therefore I would argue that anonymysed screening should occur with public knowledge but without individual explicit and specific consent. This must include the possibility of refusal, but this is likely to be exceptional.

This then is the essential moral problem of anonymysed testing. Gillon (1989) has written persuasively about the need for informed consent in all clinical research, and there remains an inescapable moral dilemma. As we will see, this is not an isolated choice.

Other ethical concerns

We have seen that there are ethical issues in anonymous testing, but there is no simple way out of this. It would be wrong to underestimate the serious- ness of the infection and how essential it is to obtain information about spread and prevalence. Those involved in public health and health planning have an ethical obligation to establish this information, in the best way scientifically and to act on it. It seems a strange ethical solution simply to do nothing; to operate, as Kennedy (1987) suggested as one alternative, 'somewhat in the blind'.

If information is to be gathered by voluntary, attributable testing then this is expensive and means that other aspects of research or service may be deprived, which also has an ethical dimension. The data obtained are likely to be of poor value epidemiologically because of participation bias.

It is therefore wrong to focus only on one aspect of ethics—such as the ownership of her discarded blood by the patient—without consideration of the broader framework of ethical issues surrounding the subject.

Bayer et al (1986) discussed the ethical issues in evaluating HIV antibody screening in the United States, where it was concluded that, referring to anonymysed prevalence studies, 'neither voluntariness nor privacy seemed threatened'. Bayer (1989) recently commented on the opinions of Kennedy and others, and the decision of the UK Social Services Committee against anonymysed screening. 'This represents a tragic misapplication of ethical principles in the face of the AIDS epidemic. There are no ethical grounds for opposing such studies. The rights of privacy do not preclude them; nor does the moral responsibility to warn the infected prevent the discovery of epidemiological patterns that are critical for the fashioning of broad public policy initiatives'.

CONCLUSIONS

I will now summarise what I think is an appropriate, and ethically reasonable approach to testing and screening for HIV in pregnancy. Underlying this is the belief that it is important to separate clinical testing, from population screening, but that surveillance must incorporate both sources.

There are now definite advantages in a woman knowing that she is HIV positive and ante-natal women should have the opportunity of being tested after full explanation with informed consent, and with pre and post test counselling. How vigorously this programme should be pursued must depend on prevalence. It may be reasonable, where prevalence is low (say 0.1% or less) to continue to offer testing on a selective or case finding basis as recommended by the Royal College of Obstetricians and Gynaecologists (1987). However, it should also be open to any woman to have testing without declaring any risk activity, once she has understood the nature of the test. The situation is different where the prevalence is high (say 0.5% or more). Here I believe we should go further and should offer counselling and suggest testing to all women as a routine part of ante-natal care. This has resource implications. Testing must still be with informed consent, and women must be assured that if they decline testing this will not affect their further care in any way.

The problem at present is that we do not have prevalence data. Without this it is difficult to plan screening at a local level and to assess how effective case selection is. At a local and national level it is difficult to provide accurate mathematical modelling and prediction of the development of the epidemic. There are further implications for planning public health, education campaigns and provision of health care facilities. Screening of ante-natal women is only one small part of the necessary information required, but they are an important group. The best way to collect this prevalence data is by anonymysed unlinked screening in whichever geographical areas are thought epidemiologically to provide the most information—the equivalent of the US sentinel areas. This should be done with public awareness, public discussion and explanation, but without individual counselling or individual explicit consent. The right to refuse would be accepted, but would be likely to be an exceptional occurrence. This combination of extensive voluntary, attributable testing, backed up wherever required with anonymysed unlinked screening, will provide the most useful epidemiological information. An essential final step is that this data must be effectively and speedily centralised, analysed, and published.

Finally no judgement on this issue is immutable. Testing and screening priorities will change as the epidemic changes. The need for extensive counselling will diminish as the population becomes more knowledgeable about HIV testing. However, I believe that the broad framework described will continue to apply.

After extensive debate over the last few years, the government has recently taken the initiative and announced that anonymysed unlinked studies will start in England and Wales on 15.1.90. The design of these studies has been clearly described (Gill et al 1989).

REFERENCES

Barton J J, O'Connor T M, Cannon M J et al. Prevalence of human immunodeficiency virus in a general prenatal population. Am. J. Obstet. Gynecol. 1989, 160, 1316–1324
Bayer R, Levine E, Wolf S M. HIV antibody screening: an ethical framework for evaluating proposal programmes. JAMA, 1986, 256, 1768–1774
Bayer R. Ethical and social policy issues raised by HIV screening: the epidemic evolves and so do the challenges. AIDS, 1989, 3, 119–124
Becker M M, Joseph J G. AIDS and behavioural change to reduce risk: a review. Am. J. Public Health, 1988, 78, 394–410
Black D, Bodmer W, Cox D et al. HIV testing on all pregnant women (letter). Lancet, 1987, ii, 1277
Blanche S, Rouxioux C, G'uihard Moscato M L et al. A prospective study of infants born to women seropositive for human immunodeficiency virus type 1. N. Eng. J. Med. 1989, 320, 1634–1648
Blendon R J, Donelan K. Discrimination against people with AIDS. The Public's perspective. N. Eng. J. Med. 1988, 319, 1022–1026
Brandt R. AIDS in historical perspective: four lessons from the history of sexually transmitted diseases. Am. J. Public Health, 1988, 78, 367–371
Brattebo G, Wiseborg T. HIV monitoring of pregnant women. Lancet, 1988, i, 713–714

Brossard Y, Goudeau A, Larsen M et al. A sero-epidemiological study of HIV in 15,465 pregnant women screened in Paris area between February 1987 and October 1987. IV International Conference on AIDS (1988). Abstract No 4632, Book 2 p. 219

Burke D S, Brundage J F, Redfield R R et al. Measurement of the false positive rate in a screening programme for human immunodeficiency virus infections. N. Eng. J. Med. 1988, 319, 961–964

Cates W jr, Handsfield H H. HIV Counselling and Testing: Does it work? Am. J. Public Health, 1988, 78, 1533–1534

CDC (1987) Public Health Service guidelines for counselling and antibody testing to prevent HIV infection and AIDS. MMWR, 1987, 36, 509–515

CDC (1988) MMWR 1988, 36, 833–845

Connor E, Goode L, Morrison S et al. Seroprevalence of human immunodeficiency virus (HIV) of parturients at University Hospital, New Jersey, USA. IV International Conference on AIDS, Abstract No 685, book 1, p. 375 1988

Des Jarlais Don C, Friedman S R. HIV infection among intravenous drug users: Epidemiology and risk reduction. AIDS, 1987, 1, 67–76

Dickens B M. Legal Rights and Duties in the AIDS epidemic. Science, 1988, 239, 580–586

Doll R A proposal for doing prevalence studies of AIDS. Br. Med. J. 1987, 294, 244

Duff P. Prenatal screening for human immunodeficiency virus infection: purpose, priorities, and pitfalls. Obstet. Gynaecol, 1989, 74, 403–404

Dyer C. Another judgement on testing for HIV without consent. Br. Med. J. 1988, 296, 1791

Eickhoff T C. Hospital policies on HIV antibody testing. JAMA, 1988, 259, 1861–1862

Entwhistle C C, Selkon J B. HIV testing on all pregnant women. Lancet 1988, i, 421

European Collaborative Study. Mother to child transmission of HIV. Lancet 1988, ii, 1039–1042

Francis D P, Chin J. The prevention of acquired immunodeficiency syndrome in the United States. JAMA, 1987, 257, 1357–1366

Gill O N, Adler M W, Day N E. Monitoring the prevalence of HIV. Br. Med. J. 1989, 299, 1295–1298

Gillett G. HIV and the Epidemiologist. Lancet 1989, ii, 1228–1229

Gillon R. Testing for HIV without permission. Br. Med. J. 1987, 294, 821–823

Gillon R. Medical treatment, medical research and informed consent. J. Med. Ethics 1989, 15, 3–5

Glover L, Miller D. Counselling in the context of HIV infection and disease. In AIDS a Pocket Book of Diagnosis and Management. Ed A Mindel Publ. Edward Arnold, 1989, Chapter 14, p. 202–220

Glynn A A. Should AIDS be notifiable? Lancet 1987, ii, 750

Healy D S, Howard T S. Reactivity to non-viral proteins on Western blot mistaken for reactivity to HIV glycoproteins. AIDS, 1989, 3, 545–546

Heath R B, Grint P C A, Hardiman A E. Anonymous testing of women attending antenatal clinics for evidence of infection with HIV. Lancet, 1988, i, 1394

Hoff R. Seroprevalence of human immunodeficiency virus among childbearing women: estimation by testing samples of blood from newborns. N. Eng. J. Med. 1988, 318, 525–530

Holman S, Berthaud M, Sunderland A et al. Women infected with human immunodeficiency virus: counselling and testing during pregnancy. Seminars in Perinatalogy, 1989a, 13, 7–15

Holman S, Sunderland A, Berthaud M et al. Prenatal HIV Counselling and Testing. Clin. Obst. Gynaecol. 1989b, 32

Horsburgh C R Jr., Ou C Y, Jason J et al. Duration of human immunodeficiency virus infection before detection of antibody. Lancet 1989, ii, 637–640

Howard L C, Hawkins D A, Marwood E et al. Transmission of human immunodeficiency virus by heterosexual contact with reference to antenatal screening. B. J. Obstet. Gynaecol. 1989. 86, 135–139

Howie P W. Evidence to the Social Services Committee. 3rd Report Problems associated with AIDS, 1987, HMSO

Howie P W. Antenatal HIV screening—ethical considerations. In AIDS and Obstetrics and Gynaecology. Proceedings of the Nineteenth Study Group of the R.C.O.G. Eds C N Hudson and F Sharp, Pub. RCOG, 1988, p. 127–132

Hudson C N, Howie P W, Beard R W. HIV testing on all pregnant women. Lancet 1988, i, 239

Hull H F, Bettinger C J, Gallaher M M et al. Comparison of HIV antibody prevalence in patients consenting to and declining HIV—antibody testing in a STD clinic. JAMA, 1988, 260, 935–938

Imagawa D T, Lee M M, Wolinsky S M et al. Human immunodeficiency virus type 1 infection in homosexual men who remain seronegative for prolonged periods. N. Eng. J. Med. 1989, 320, 1458–1462

Italian Multicentre Study. Epidemiology, clinical features, and prognostic factors of paediatric HIV infection. Lancet, 1988, ii, 1043–1045

James M E. HIV positivity diagnosed during pregnancy: Psychosocial characterization of patients and their adaptation. Gen. Hosp. Psychiatry, 1988, 10, 309

Johnstone F D, MacCallum L R, Brettle R P et al. Testing for HIV in Pregnancy: 3 years Experience in Edinburgh City. Scottish Med. J. 1989, 34, 561–563

Johnstone F D, Brettle R P, MacCallum L R et al. Women's knowledge of their HIV antibody state: its effect on their decision whether to continue the pregnancy. Br. Med. J. 1990, 300, 23–24

Kennedy I. Problems associated with AIDS. 3rd report. Social Services Committee 1987, HMSO

Kirby M. The New AIDS Virus: Ineffective and unjust laws. J. AIDS 1988, 1, 304–312

Krasinski K, Borkowsky W, Bebenroth D, Moore T. Failure of voluntary testing for human immunodeficiency virus to identify infected parturient women in a high risk population. N. Eng. J. Med. 1988, 318, 185

Lancet Editorial. Clinical Trials of Zidovudine in HIV infection. Lancet, 1989, ii, 484

Landesman S, Minkoff H, Holman S et al. Serosurvey of human immunodeficiency virus infection in parturients. Implications for human immunodeficiency virus testing programmes of pregnant women. JAMA, 1987, 258, 2701

Lindsay M K, Peterson H B, Feng T I et al. Routine antepartum human immunodeficiency infection screening in an inner city population. Obstet. Gynaecol. 1989, 74, 289–294

Lo B, Steinbrook R L, Cooke M et al. Voluntary screening for human immunodeficiency virus infection: weighing the benefits and harms. Ann. Intern. Med. 1989, 110, 727–733

Lucas A. In discussion. AIDS and Obstetrics and Gynaecology. Proceedings of the Nineteenth Study Group of the Royal College of Obstetricians and Gynaecologists. Published R.C.O.G. 1988, 133–134

MacDonald I. Problems associated with AIDS. 3rd report. Social Services Committee 1987, HMSO

Marteau T M. Psychological costs of screening. Br. Med. J. 1989, 299, 527

Minkoff H, Landesman S H. The case for routinely offering prenatal testing for human immunodeficiency virus. Am. J. Obst. Gynecol, 1988, 159, 793–796

Minkoff H L, de Regt R H, Landesman S et al. Pneumocystis carinii pneumonia associated with acquired immunodeficiency syndrome in pregnancy: a report of three maternal deaths. Obstetrics and Gynaecology 1986, 67, 284–287

Mortimer J Y. The influence of assay sensitivity and specificity on error rates in three anti-HIV testing strategies. AIDS 1989, 3, 199–207

Orr A. Legal AIDS: Implications of AIDS and HIV for British and American law. J. Med. Ethics. 1989, 15, 61–67

Ou C Y, Kwok S, Mitchell S W et al. DNA amplification for direct detection of HIV 1 in DNA of peripheral blood mononuclear cells. Science 1988, 239, 295–297

Pezzella M, Rossi P, Lombardi V et al. HIV viral sequences in seronegative people at risk detected by in situ hybridisation and polymerase chain reaction. Br. Med. J. 1989, 298, 713–716

Quinn T C, Glasser D, Cannon R O et al. Human immunodeficiency virus infection among patients attending clinics for sexually transmitted disease. N. Eng. J. Med. 1987, 318, 197–203

Ranki A, Valle S L, Krohn M et al. Long latency precedes overt seroconversion in sexually transmitted human-immunodeficiency virus infection. Lancet 1987, ii, 589–593

RCOG. Report of the Royal College of Obstetricians and Gynaecologists Sub-Committee on Problems Associated with AIDS in Relation to Obstetrics and Gynaecology. RCOG 1987, London

Rhame F S, Maki D G. The case for wider use of testing for HIV infection. N. Eng. J. Med. 1989, 320, 1248–1254

Ryder R W, Nsa W, Hassig S E et al. Perinatal transmission of the human immunodeficiency virus type 1 to infants of seropositive women in Zaire. N. Eng. J. Med. 1989, 320, 1637–1642

Selwyn P A, Carter R J, Schoenbaum E E et al. Knowledge of HIV antibody status and decision to continue or terminate pregnancy among intravenous drug users. JAMA 1989, 261, 3567–3571

Sherer R. Physician use of the HIV antibody test. JAMA, 1988, 259, 264–265

Sherr L, Victor C, Stevens A. The psychological cost of HIV screening in antenatal clinics. In Les Implications du SIDA pour la mere et l'enfant. Paris, 27/30 November 1989. Abstract, D16, p. 109

Sherrard M, Gatt I. Human Immunodeficiency Virus (HIV) antibody testing. Br. Med. J. 1987, 295, 911–912

Social Services Committee. Problems associated with AIDS. 3rd Report, May 1987, HMSO

Sperling R S, Sacks H S, Mayer L et al. Umbilical cord serosurvey for human immuno-deficiency virus in parturient women in a voluntary hospital in New York City. Obstet. Gynaecol. 1989, 73, 179–181

Stevens A, Victor C, Sherr L, Beard R. HIV Testing in Antenatal Clinics: The impact on women. AIDS Care, 1989, 1, 165–171

Thornton J G. HIV Testing of Pregnant Women. Lancet, 1987, ii, 1530

Van Griensven G J P, de Vroome E M M, Tielman R A P et al. Impact of HIV antibody testing on changes in sexual behaviour among homosexual men in the Netherlands. Am. J. Public Health, 1988, 78, 1575–1577

Volberding P. HIV infection as a Disease: The medical indications for early diagnosis. J. of Acquired Immune Deficiency Syndrome, 1989, 2, 421–425

Weiss R, Thier So. HIV testing is the answer: what's the question? N. Eng. J. Med. 1988, 319, 1010–1012

WHO Global Programme on AIDS. Unlinked anonymous screening for the public health surveillance of HIV infections. Proposed international guidelines. Geneva WHO 1989

Summary and observations

16. The discussion reviewed

G. R. Dunstan

It is not for the last speaker to outline or to summarise the earlier presentations. That would be both tedious and superfluous. Rather he should recall into awareness some of the ethical assumptions explicit or implicit in what has been said.

The subject of the symposium is Reproductive Medicine and the Law. The papers leave no one complacent. No hearer of them could rest assured that whether as a guide to medical practice or as a public safeguard the law and its practice are the best that can be devised. The uncertainties of the law are many. Doctors may complain that they are put thereby at continual risk. Yet when certainties are contemplated, the question is raised, Do we really want them? What sort of degree of certainty is possible in an art—*techne* is the word for it in Hippocrates— grounded in an ever-developing science and practised upon human beings who all partake of the biological random and variability of nature with infinite personal idiosyncracies as well? Or consider the law of delict/tort, as its working was illustrated by Symonds and Cameron in the last session. The necessity and nature of proof, both of causation and of negligence, impose prolonged uncertainty on complainant and doctor alike*; and the award of damages, when left to a jury, seems to lack all reasonable consistency both in *quantum* and in methods of payment. No worse example of the rule of law in medicine could be imagined.

Why, then, is the law involved with medicine at all? Granted that it is the doctor's professional duty to serve the patient's perceived interests to the best of his ability, why should he not be free to do so, governed only by the patient's consent? The question was raised in Baird's and Norrie's treatment of contragestion, action to prevent the implantation of the blastocyst, and of menstrual regulation, which involves dislodging it soon after it has implanted. Granted the uncertainties involved, about when a pregnancy has begun, and about an intervenor's intention, and about which law is in question, and granted the obvious advantage to the mother of interruption of the pregnancy (if that is what it is) very early rather than later, why should the law be concerned with her treatment? Why, it was asked later,

---

* See Appendix Note, p. 149.

should the law be concerned with selective feticide when one twin manifests a defect, or with the reduction of a high-order multiple pregnancy? In both instances, it could be alleged, the intervention is in the interest of the mother and of the surviving children—and, indeed, of the otherwise potentially-overloaded local services for neonatal care. What concern is it of the law?

Already as the questions are asked, pointers to an answer become clear. The law is concerned with a balance of related interests; it is concerned to see that the serving of one is not at the expense of others equally legitimate. In the last instance, the fetus has an interest in that it embodies a human life with a presumption in its favour—it is a life which we have a *prima facie* duty to protect. The public has an interest in the efficient use of its limited health resources. It has also an interest in keeping that presumption in favour of human life unless and until that presumption is rebutted for grave and weighty reasons.

The same point was reached in the discussion of abortion. Norrie alleged that the purpose of abortion legislation is to protect the pregnant woman from harm: the strict offence created by the Offences Against the Person Act 1861 drove women to the illegal 'backstreet' abortionist and so put them at grave physical risk; to permit abortion for stated indications lessened that risk. (It would follow, he said, that to oppose, on allegedly moral grounds, contragestion or interference with the recently-implanted embryo would be to frustrate that beneficent purpose of the law, since the risks of termination increased with gestational age.)

Historically, of course, the reasons for making abortion a 'crime', first under the canon law, triable in the spiritual or church courts, and then, since 1803, by statute, were: abortion robbed the state of a potential able body to do the state's necessary work—tilling, making, trading, fighting; abortion was a sinful resort, to cover up earlier, causative, sins; and, above all, it was an invasion of that basic principle of the common morality, the protection due to innocent life, the presumption in its favour.

Can we afford to cheapen that presumption, or to let it go? Utilitarian considerations apart (and to recollect the political butcheries of 1989 is to recall how weighty those considerations are), innocent life found in the company two determined defenders. Simmonds cried out against the notion that doctors might destroy some to save some—the strong in a drifting lifeboat might throw the weak overboard in order that the strong might survive: there is a fundamental *wrong* in selective feticide unless the mother is clearly at risk. This was the utterance of an intuitive moral judgment: a sense of moral repugnance without which man as we know him would be no longer man—he would be morally insensitive, imbecile, impoverished. The adverse side of intuitive judgment came out later when those cultures were recalled which preferred males to females and so would encourage the survival of the one and discourage, to say the least, the survival of the other. But that adverse factor is not sufficient to impugn the value of intuitive moral judgment in principle—the sense of sheer wrong—provided that it is capable of reasoned exposition and support.

Gormally brought to Simmonds's protest precisely that support, with the appeal to natural justice ingrained in Western moral philosophy. What underlies our concept of justice is the quality of all human beings, our mere humanity. If we differentiate on the basis of acquired abilities or disabilities, we move to a matter of choice, whom we treat justly or not. Justice depends on intentional acts. Sometimes foreseen consequences must be lived with, if they cannot be removed without chosen injustice. Selective reduction *is* repugnant, and for these reasons.

But the question is not thereby closed. Simmonds's sense of repugnance is balanced by that of others against doing nothing when action could prevent an ill: inaction might be a wrong, even though (following Boyd) they might live with a sense of guilt for the means which they felt bound to employ. (Boyd did not say in which sense he used the word 'guilt', whether that of moral culpability or that of psychological trauma; but the point need not be pursued.) Gormally's position is similarly assailable. He asserted a strict principle—the inviolability of innocent life. (He too did not stay to spell out the meaning of 'innocent' in this context. Historically it cannot always be taken to mean what it is now commonly assumed to mean, that is, morally blameless. Etymologically, and in the historic moral tradition, 'innocent' means doing no harm, or seriously threatening none. So a soldier armed, who may be morally blameless of the war, may lawfully be shot; but once disarmed or disabled, his life is protected, for he can do no further harm, whatever his moral character may be.) Gormally, then, alleged a strict principle, with the latent ambiguity unresolved. But in the common morality, and in the realities of practice, we are seldom at liberty to derive a strict duty—that is an absolute, unexceptional, obligation—from a strict principle. The reason for this is that ethical questions of real difficulty stand, most often, at the meeting point of a cluster of principles, each stating its own claim; and when those claims collide, choices have to be made. We may not, however, choose to ignore Gormally's stand on principle any more than we may ignore Simmonds's intuitive sense of wrong. Without that stand, without that stake deeply fixed in the common morality, there could be no strain, no ethical tension, in the choices to which we are driven. Without the constant claims and restraints of justice, our humanity would be diminished and society would be without moral sinew.

We cannot dispense with the presumption in favour of life, or with the presumptive duty to protect life. Choices have to be made when indications of such gravity arise as to challenge that presumption. The whole of today's discussion presupposes that, in law, as in morals, there are in practice indications of such gravity as to rebut that presumption, to permit the taking of pre-embryonic, embryonic or fetal life. In those choices a calculation of foreseeable consequence necessarily has a part. We have, then, identified three elements in the process of moral decision: the first, intuition; the second, the appeal, *a priori*, a governing principle laid down, it could be said, by religion or by moral reasoning; the third, the estimation of consequence. None may be ignored.

Not the least of the service given by Norrie was his elucidation of the difficulties in determining when the presumption of a protectable life begins. Given present knowledge, protectable status must be attributed: it is not biologically and observably 'given'. If the old laws of abortion required an assumption about when pregnancy begins, the new laws now being fashioned to govern research and practice before pregnancy, that is, with the pre-embryonic cells in vitro, require some assumption about the status of those cells. The absolutist who attributes to them the fully-protected status claimed for the human person can do so only by ignoring three sets of data: the lack of individuality in those cells while they are still fluid and uncommitted; the requirement in Western philosophy and moral tradition of individuality—of an organic homogeneous whole—as a necessity for the embodiment of personality, moral, legal or psycho-somatic; and a tradition of two and a half thousand years' duration, maintained by Western philosophy and Christianity alike, which increased the protection due *pari passu* with fetal growth towards maturity. (In fact, the tradition can be traced further back in history and more widely in other cultures; but that need not be pursued now.) In the language of Aristotelian philosophy and science, protection began when the fetus was *formatus*— visibly formed into a human shape—and therefore supposedly *animatus*, formed into that shape by the *psyche* (*anima*) of a rational human being. And that, they said, occurred at upwards of forty days—a point of determination accepted by Roman Catholic moral theology, canon law and casuistry until 1869. In the language of the common law, protection was legally afforded at quickening—by an understandable transition when the philosophical term *animatus* became identified with the subjective, maternal experience of *vivificatus*, quickening, the first stirring of life in the womb. (Dunstan & Seller 1988, Ford & Norman 1988). Legislators now who are inclined to settle for the point when individual embryogenesis begins with the primitive streak are working within the same tradition; only they are bringing the time back from day-forty plus to day-fourteen.

Such a law would bring the implanted embryo under the protection of the Abortion Acts. It would not thereby dismiss the pre-embryonic cells as of no account. Following the Warnock principle, it would mark its recognition of their being of genetically human stock by setting limits and conditions to govern in vitro research and therapeutic manipulation. It does not do so for any non-human pre-embryonic cells.

There was in discussion an inadvertent slip of the tongue, I think, when it was said that the embryo 'became part of the mother' when she and the early blastocyst began to exchange signals. Can this really be so? Are there not here *two* lives, one lodged within and dependent on the other, in a relational dependency which will change in form throughout pregnancy and birth and even after birth? The purpose of the law, Mrs Pickup said (I believe rightly), is to protect the fetus while protecting the interests of the mother. Once the concept of two lives is lost, the possibility of protection is lost with it, except under the law of mayhem, self-mutilation; and the question of personality cannot arise. A serious maternal interest may be threatened by the growing fetus, just as the interest of the fetus may be threatened by the mother's irresponsible behaviour. The whole ethics of their relation, and of permissible intervention, rests on this balance of inter-related interests. An abortion cannot properly be reduced to maternal self-mutilation. The doctor—be he. obstetrician, paediatrician or general medical adviser—cannot escape this complex of interests. He has to weigh their respective claims, having in mind his general obligation to serve the patient by means which risk or impose minimal harm, and, at the same time, to have regard to the common good and its intrinsic interest in a strong presumption in favour of human life.

Statutes like the Abortion Act and the Infant Life Preservation Act give particular direction to the common law duty to protect innocent human life. The Human Fertilisation and Embryology Bill will add to their number. That prospect raises again the quest for certainties. Opponents of regulated research on human pre-embryonic cells assume a scientific certainty which does not exist, and seek a legalistic certainty attainable, if at all, only at the cost of restricting the duty (as well as the liberty) of scientific enquiry and the therapeutic application of its results. The Archbishop of York, in a notable television interview, asked his interrogator 'Has it ever occurred to you that the lust for certainty may itself be a sin?' He received no answer. Conventional wisdom would prefer, within the framework of law, and under principled supervision, professional self-regulation: that is, regulation by the professional conscience of the scientists and practitioners concerned. That conscience is, first, a corporate one, held in common by the profession, and exercised personally by its members. Its existence comes to the public notice more sharply in the occasional breach of duty than in its general exercise. It operates today under more external scrutiny than before, not only because of invasive media attention, but also through lay participation in research ethics committees and the like. The personal conscience of the doctor is more open to the eddies and tides of popular sentiment and social pressure than before, because he is a member of a morally restless society, concerned, yet wavering and uncertain in the direction of its concern. To seek refuge in certainties is a tempting short-cut to safety when so much is diffuse.

Moreover, where credible approaches to certainty are available, it is a professional duty to conform with them. The grave problems of high order multiple pregnancies would be markedly reduced by rigorous hormonal monitoring—by established tests—in ovarian stimulation, and by restraint in the number of gametes and pre-embryos replaced in assisted conception.

Failure in the one, and a flouting of commonly-accepted guidelines in the other, result in bizarre episodes which discredit professional credibility in the public eye. They fuel the demand for restrictive, statutory control, as do well-publicised instances of a too-ready disposal of problematical neonatal life. So would the trivialising of selective reduction of pregnancy or of abortion to assure a child of the desired sex. The price to be paid for discretion is prudence.

It may be politically necessary, given the present conflicts of opinion, to put bench-marks into legislation to give at least the appearance of certainties. Such a provision would be a clause in a statute specifying 14 days from the mixing of the gametes as the term dividing permitted from criminal manipulations. This date is commonly accepted by embryologists as the time when the primitive streak has appeared. Scientists are unlikely to claim it as a certainty; it is a working hypothesis which future experience may either confirm, modify or falsify. It would seem to me to be a mistake to entrench even a working hypothesis into the terms of a statute as the ground of distinction between lawful and criminal activity. The mistake was made, in relation to viability, in the Infant Life Preservation Act 1929. It has proved very difficult to change the presumption of viability to accord with subsequently developed medical practice. So it may be with the 14 day rule. It would seem to me better to write some general principle about protectable status into the statute, and lay upon the statutory licensing authority a duty to embody that principle in rules apt to the state of knowledge as it exists or develops over time.

Such a proposal encounters at once the riposte of the 'slippery slope': that, unless barred by statute, researchers will always press for more and more time. The riposte presupposes first, that there is a strong scientific interest in extending permitted time and a will among scientists to do so; and secondly, that the scientists and the members of the licensing authority are so lacking in integrity and common prudence as to extend that date improperly, regardless of all moral and social indications to the contrary. Those presuppositions may be doubted.

Law is necessarily a conservative force. In the face of change, it can buy time for change to prove its value, or to be tested as a force disruptive of other protectable interests. (To admit this is not to justify the intolerable delays in delict/tort litigation after some medical mishap; those have other causes.) But the professional conscience is also a conservative force. Lethargy alone cannot account for the observed distance between some medical practice and relevant medical research. Neither can the factor of learning time. We may regret, for instance, the gap between the control of pain, and of distress in terminal care in contexts where the benefits of up-to-date pharmacology and sensitive nursing skills are given to patients and where nothing better is offered than the crude stunning which was all that could be offered in an obsolete past. Time is required for what is taught to new student generations to get back to those qualified in the past. But ethical conservatism is of a different sort. If a clinician's first duty is the service of his patient, he has to assure himself that what is newly offered is better than what he could offer before. The medical researcher and the clinical innovator have to prove their point. The same could be said of the keeping of medical secrets. It may not be easy for one imbued with the tradition of one-to-one confidence to accept that the new practice of medical genetics, for instance, requires the sharing of confidences within families in which deleterious genes can be traced. A too stubborn stance on secrecy can result in avoidable harm. Yet the strong tendencies towards a State autocracy in Britain today make it all the more imperative that medicine remains firm, conservative, in its tenacity to the primacy of the individual patient. In other words, a professional cherishing of moral certainties could offer the public better assurance than illusory legal certainties, imposed by statute. (The extent to which such moral certainties can be absolute, dictating strict or absolute duties irrespective of other interests and considerations, need not be pursued here.)

In short, a symposium on Reproductive Law and Medicine was aptly concluded by Sheila McLean with the remark that 'we aim for consistencies, not for certainties.' Her words recalled in one mind those of the Psalmist: *judicia Domini vera, justificata in semetipsa.*

REFERENCES

Dunstan G R, Seller M J (1988) ed. The Status of the Human Embryo: Perspectives from moral tradition. London: Oxford University Press for King Edward's Hospital Fund for London. See especially chapter 5, The human embryo in the western moral tradition
Ford Norman M (1988) When did I Begin? Conception of the human individual in history, philosophy and science. Cambridge: Cambridge University Press

APPENDED NOTE

It was suggested that, because evidences became more uncertain with time, medical and nursing staff should meet after a problematical case and record relevant facts and judgments for future possible use. Thomas Percival touched on the subject in his *Medical Ethics*, 1803, s. XXVIII: He imposed on 'the gentlemen of the faculty' the duty at the close of every interesting and important case, especially fatal ones, calmly to review and reflect upon the management of it, without self-deception. 'Regrets may follow, but criminality will be thus obviated. For good intentions and the imperfections of human skill which cannot anticipate the knowledge that events alone disclose, will sufficiently justify what is past, provided the failure is made conscientiously subservient to future wisdom and rectitude in professional conduct.'

Thomas Percival, *Medical Ethics*: or a code of Institutes and Precepts adapted to the Professional Conduct of Physicians and Surgeons (1803). Ed. Chaunay D Leake. Baltimore: T Williams, Wilkins Coy., 1927.

17. The control of reproductive research

M. Donaldson

When I accepted the kind invitation to speak at this conference, I had no idea it would lead to my giving the plenary lecture. I have never given a lecture before in my life. I am not sure whether I am taking on the role of a Daniel in the den of lions or a Daniel come to judgement. In either case, I find myself as a complete non-academic, a lay person with no medical or scientific qualifications, having the temerity to address an audience of professionals on their own subject.

As technology has advanced, so medical and scientific knowledge has grown and developed with ever-increasing rapidity. This has accelerated over the past decade. Even 25 years ago in our London teaching hospitals, the consultant was still a god-like figure going his rounds with his attendant acolytes. Patients were cases, often routine, sometimes interesting, and the doctor always knew best. Gradually amidst the many social changes, alas, not all for the better, came the need to know, together with the patient's right to be fully informed. The press, the radio and newspapers had a field day. Every new medical advance was fully discussed and written about, even shown in minute detail on television screens. Strict accuracy and factual information in many cases played second fiddle to drama and titillation. Patients were persuaded to reveal their problems, worries and their case histories. Doctors appeared and discussed different treatments and the whole wonderful mystique of the medical world was opened up. Finally, Louise Brown arrived.

Once the wonder and delight at this breakthrough had been exhausted, the public were ready to fear the worst that science could inflict upon them. Here were a group of doctors and scientists who could apparently create life in a test tube. Do you remember those articles headed by a picture of a baby sitting in the top of a tube? We knew that in the animal world species could be cross-bred to improve production. A master race was no longer science fiction. Cloning was possible, and why not further cross-fertilisation of a human egg? Why should not we all pre-determine the sex of our children? Why not rid ourselves of the physically weak and disabled and severely mentally retarded before birth? Why not pre-select those who should be born and leave others to perish? These and other ethical questions were the subject of media speculation and public concern.

Finally in 1982, the Government intervened. As in all situations where it is not quite sure what to do, it set up a Committee. This committee under the chairmanship of Baroness Warnock, as she now is, reported in 1984, its main recommendation being that there should be a statutory licensing authority to regulate both research and certain specified infertility services. Again the media had material for an unending series of articles and programmes. Pressure groups sprang up for and against the Report's findings. There was the famous or infamous Powell Bill for the protection of the unborn child, seeking to forbid all research on the human embryo, which fell, but only by a parliamentary manoeuvre. The Government realising what a hot political potato it now had on its hands did nothing.

In 1985, the Royal College of Obstetricians and Gynaecologists and the Medical Research Council decided jointly to sponsor an Authority exactly along the lines recommended by the Warnock Committee. As obviously it couldn't be a statutory body, they decided, and in retrospect I feel unfortunately, to call it the Voluntary Licensing Authority, 'voluntary' meaning that centres could decide whether or not they wanted to be licensed. I say 'unfortunately', because in the minds of just a few, it conjured up visions of well-meaning, uninformed volunteers seeking to control this very difficult medical field. I was asked to be the lay chairman of a combined professional and lay authority.

The composition of the lay membership has been criticised. It has been suggested that the addition of a past patient might be advantageous. In fact, among our lay members we have both a past patient and those whose own families have suffered from the problems of infertility. It was also inferred that we would be unduly influenced by our professional members and would tend blindly to accept their views. This has never been the case.

It is a remarkable fact that this originally disparate group of professional and lay members has for over four years remained an almost constant entity, the only change in our composition being the loss of three members due to a change in their personal circumstances and the addition of extra members to cope with the great increase in our work. We now number nine professionals and nine lay members and meet as an Authority every other month. The visits to centres, working parties to discuss special issues, and attendance at our own and other conferences somehow get fitted in between, for, and this is often not realised, except for our secretariat, we are a completely unpaid body. Very busy professional and lay people give an enormous amount of time and effort to our work. We are now generally accepted by both the centres and the public as the regulating authority. We have willingly continued with our work three years longer than was anticipated. The Department of Health, having since our formation adopted a completely neutral stance towards our efforts, has now acknowledged them by way of a small grant of £40 000.

If I were being cynical, I might wonder if our willingness to continue as an Authority and the Government's recognition of our work was not part of their reluctance to hasten legislation—a Statutory Licensing Authority being a much more expensive alternative—but in fairness, it is, as I have said, a political hot potato and full of ethical minefields.

Before our first meeting, I well remember wondering what on earth had we taken on. I did express doubts as to whether those consultants who by now had attained considerable expertise and public recognition would in fact accept any form of regulation or control from this outside and unproven non-statutory body. I think it reflects very well on all those dealing with this most delicate emotional and often controversial subject of infertility that all centres responded. We were invited to come and see their work and to license them. Some were obviously more willing than others, but initially all agreed with our guidelines.

We found ourselves faced with a dual role, that of a monitoring authority and that of a public watchdog and interpreter. During those first months as an Authority, the lay members were themselves involved in a learning process. Our professional colleagues for their part were faced, possibly for the first time, with questioning in some depth. They were asked to explain and to justify any treatment advocated by our centres and to explain the exact methods used and the benefits which might accrue from any proposed research project. We found ourselves becoming conversant with an entirely new vocabulary. In this context, we spent much time over what terminology should be adopted when referring to the fertilised egg before its multiplying cells had produced a primitive streak. It has been alleged that this search for new terminology was a deliberate attempt by some research scientists to fudge the issue of when life begins. As far as our Authority was concerned it was at the request of the lay members that some form of terminology was sought, some word which would convey the fact that whilst there was potential for human life, until that primitive streak is formed its certainty was not determined. We discussed whether 'conceptus' or 'pre-embryo' was the more acceptable. It was decided, again by the lay members, who represent the public view, that 'pre-embryo' was a term the public would more readily understand. It is an interesting fact that the American Fertility Society Ethics Committee were quite independently also seeking terminology. In 1986, they arrived at exactly the same choice having in their case deliberated between pro and pre-embryo. The RCOG has just recently decided to adopt 'pre-embryo' when discussing what was previously known as the pre-implantation conceptus. So I do hope that in the coming debate on legislation this accusation of fudging the issue will not be repeated.

We had to decide how we would undertake this task of licensing centres. Many were already involved in work which statutorily required no licence and had no obligation to conform to any guidance and directive. A programme of visits was organised. Small teams from the Authority, usually three, including at least one lay member, made the initial visit. At the following meeting of the whole Authority, the results of each visit were reported and the findings discussed. Gradually, an acceptable protocol or model emerged of what were the desirable minimum standards we would accept for licensing. Centres who didn't reach these standards were notified of any defects we felt existed or improvements which should be made and a return visit offered before they were accepted on to our approved list of centres.

We now expect centres to meet the following requirements:

—The clinician in charge should be of consultant status or there should be one available for overall supervision who would take responsibility for the running of the centre.

—There should be back-up facilities—by this we mean the necessary hospital facilities for treatment in the event of an emergency. In very early days, we asked one clinician working in very cramped and unsuitable conditions what would he do in an emergency. He replied 'Dial 999.' Fortunately, those days are long past.

—There should be an adequate laboratory with trained and experienced technicians.

—All human gametes should be stored and incubated in separate and fully labelled and identified containers. There should be safe storage for frozen materials.

—There should be a consent form for treatment of an approved format.

—Files on patients should be kept secure and confidential.

—Ethics committees should be conversant with the treatment offered and should meet regularly with those working in the centres.

—In addition, ideally, independent counselling services should be available to help couples with the stress and frustration they suffer. This is an ideal which we accept cannot always be met through the lack of trained counsellors.

There has been a question as to how sure we can be that we really know what is going on in all our centres and research establishments. The late Professor Ian Donald speaking to MPs and the press stated, 'To catch me out, any inspector would need to know as much about my work as I did.' Here, I think, we can rely on the human factor. Infertility is a comparatively small and new medical field. All working within it know each other. Nobody working in complete isolation is going to achieve any scientific or medical breakthrough or develop any new techniques. Patients, the laboratories and their staff and materials are all needed. Rumours start and spread and soon somebody would be querying the work or methods used. This has happened three times already leading ultimately to a revision of our guidelines.

As technology advanced, our guidelines needed constant revision and new ones added. This was never undertaken without wide consultation followed by discussion and a consensus approach was the one always adopted. In 1987 we amended two, one concerning the number of pre-embryos to be implanted, the other concerning egg donors. Our first controversy arose over the number of pre-embryos to be implanted during one treatment cycle. We had ample evidence, not only nationally but internationally, that the danger of multiple births was dramatically increased if four or more fertilised eggs were used in one cycle. We accordingly amended that guideline by limiting the number of pre-embryos to be implanted to three and in exceptional circumstances four. Here I would add that, from our latest statistics, it has been shown that with the improvements in technique very good results can be obtained by the implantation of two pre-embryos, and one centre is achieving comparable results by just implanting one. I would further point out that of the total of multiple births in 1987, apart from twins, IVF and GIFT treatment accounted for over 50% of the 142 sets of triplets and eight sets of quadruplets that year. Such multiple births produce babies in need of our neonatal services which are already over-stretched and do not exist in the private sector where most of these multiple births occur.

Success rates following IVF vary considerably between centres and in most large well-established centres results are inevitably better than those for the newly established and smaller ones. A successful IVF programme requires a good team with good surgery and good embryology provided by experienced embryologists: the right people with the right experience working together. Unfortunately good embryologists are in short supply which is why we welcome the initiative of Bourn Hall which actually sets out to offer this specific training.

I sometimes question whether it is every woman's inalienable right to have a child regardless of the means used to produce it and whether the future welfare of any baby is not paramount to this wish. Perhaps it was put more succinctly by Professor Harry Krause. Writing in 1985 he stated that a child is not medication to be prescribed lightly to frustrated would-be parents. Contrary to some of the views expressed, I agree with those who would offer treatment for infertility only to those married couples or those in a state of long term relationship analogous to marriage. I do not believe that single women should be accepted into a programme. The argument often voiced is that the single parent can in certain circumstances be just as acceptable as an adoptive parent. To a child already born suffering the hardship of being an orphan or abandoned, one parent may be better than none. This is quite a different situation from deliberately producing the single parent syndrome when the public acceptance is still of the two-parent family as a unit.

I would also venture to criticise some private clinics whose annual turnover of the number of women attempting to become fertile is really enormous, but whose results are still comparatively low. I know that to make a cut-off of the number of treatment cycles allowed brings added stress to the couple. As we have said, very careful and experienced counselling by an independent counsellor before embarking on any programme should be an obligatory requirement. Equally important is the follow-up counselling after failure and the help to a couple to come to a decision as to whether the price they are paying (I do not mean the financial price) is too high for them to continue with more treatment.

But to return to our amended guidelines. We circulated centres reminding them that lack of conformation with our new guidelines could lead to the Authority's approval being withdrawn. It was reported to us that one large licensed centre was implanting a large number of pre-embryos. Further, it was inferred that selective reduction was then taking place. The centre confirmed the first allegation, but disputed the second. We had much discussion with the consultants working in the centre and they insisted on their right to exercise their clinical freedom to treat their patients as they felt best. As they could not abide by our guidelines, we withdrew their licence. Being a non-statutory body, we had no means of enforcement at our disposal. In fact both the consultant concerned and the media who were following the whole saga stated we were toothless tigers. I much regret that penal sanctions may have to be introduced in the proposed legislation since the result in this case demonstrated that self-regulation, peer pressure, press publicity and resulting lack of patient confidence *can* bring about the desired result. Suffice it to say that the consultants agreed, albeit reluctantly, to abide by our new guideline and after re-visiting and further discussions with all concerned, including their ethics committee, we restored their licence.

Our second amended guideline equally caused problems and still does. It was that of egg donation. Should donors be anonymous? This was and still is a matter for debate. Sponsored by the King Edward Fund, we held an all-day conference devoted entirely to this one topic. Our speakers held passionate views both for and against anonymity, as did the participating audience. As an Authority, we discussed at great length the whole problem taking into account the views which had been expressed. The general consensus was that donors should remain anonymous. We appreciate that for some ethnic groups this can pose problems. In such cases, the centre's ethics committee can always seek guidance and they would not find the Authority unsympathetic in this, a very small minority of cases.

In December 1986, a consultation paper, *Legislation on Human Infertility Services and Embryo Research*, was widely circulated. We were asked for our comments. As far as the actual clauses covering infertility treatment were concerned, they were based on the Warnock Report. Developments since were covered by our guidelines which had been incorporated within the paper, so we were very well satisfied. We were however disturbed by the approach adopted on research. Research on a pre-embryo, that is defined in the paper as a fertilised egg up to the development of a primitive streak, or 14 days, whichever is the earlier, would depend on a free vote in Parliament. This we find very worrying. Past debates in both Houses have demonstrated a considerable degree of ignorance and misunderstanding by some

Members. Others, we accept, hold strongly-held religious views. There have been references to genetic engineering, a selection process to produce a superior breed, cloning, etc. Furthermore, as Hansard shows in reporting the debate of 16 December 1988 in the Commons, confusion was created by the unfortunate linking of the abortion reform bill with embryo research. In spite of promised legislation, this debate was followed by another in the Lords on 7 March 1989. The Duke of Norfolk's Private Member's Bill which he introduced on that day was but a carbon copy of the bill introduced by Enoch Powell in the Commons, which was defeated.

There is a very powerful lobby mounted against embryo research and it would be a tragedy if all present work were to be halted. Professor Winston at the Hammersmith Hospital has achieved a wonderful breakthrough by the determination of the sex of the very early pre-embryo. This enables doctors to prevent the birth of a child suffering from a genetically trans-mitted disease such as muscular dystrophy and haemophilia which affects only boys. Many other genetic diseases and congenital abnormalities might also be diagnosed if research is allowed to continue. It must be the ultimate decision of the parents as to whether their defective embryo should be born, whether the sanctity of creation outweighs the quality of life of the future child and its welfare. We know for a fact that more research would and could be undertaken if scientists and others were not hesitant to embark on long term projects which might suddenly be curtailed by restrictive legis-lation.

This free vote in Parliament is to be on the adoption of two alternative clauses. Clause 2 allows research under licence and strict control and Clause 1 states 'It will be a criminal offence to carry out procedures on a human embryo other than those aimed at preparing the embryo for transfer to the uterus of a woman or those carried out to ascertain the suitability of that embryo for the intended transfer'. I regret that SPUC (Society for the Protection of the Unborn Child) and the pro-life lobby have stated quite publicly their intention to produce amendments relating to abortion law reform during the debate. This is a deliberate attempt to cause confusion and designed to wreck any considered argument. It is using a parliamentary manoeuvre to bring about a result they have been unable so far to achieve. We have neither the resources nor the manpower to mount a counter-campaign, nor do I feel that as a regulating authority we should go to the hustings. Our role is to give accurate and factual information. We hope that more weight will be given to this than to emotional outbursts.

To try and inform the general public and members of both Houses we have just produced a report on all the research work undertaken since our inception. In this paper, we draw attention to the disastrous results which would follow the adoption of Clause 1. Briefly these are:

—improvements in the techniques of IVF would effectively cease;
—women undergoing any new treatment related to IVF and their pre-embryos would become experimental subjects;

—many causes of infertility would remain unknown;
—it would not be possible to develop safe and reliable techniques for pre-implantation diagnosis of genetic abnormalities;
—research on contraception involving IVF designed to alleviate the world population problem would cease.

These are some of the practical reasons why properly licensed research should be allowed to continue. One of our British scientists involved in such research, Professor Leese, stated: 'Research and advances in medicine are inseparable. Properly disciplined scientific human curiosity is a noble part of our culture. It is a sterile and dogmatic society that stifles responsible research and it is arrogant to suppose that we know enough.

As I mentioned, last year we received Government recognition in the form of a small grant of £40 000 to cover secretarial help and some of the printing costs. I have recently made a further request for financial support. In view of Government recognition and the need to emphasise the desirability of urgent legislation, we changed our name in April to that of the Interim Licensing Authority.

With the increase in the number of centres offering GIFT and with the need to visit new IVF centres and re-license old ones, we have reached a stage where we know we can now no longer function as effectively as we would wish. It is our earnest hope that next April will see our fifth and final annual report and that the new Statutory Licensing Authority will take over as speedily as possible. When the new Authority comes into being, those few of our critics who feel that our guidelines are too restrictive will discover they are able to enforce theirs with all the power of the criminal law behind them.

Legislation is needed to protect both clinicians and patients as new techniques develop. Take for example selective reduction. There is no adequate law covering this. Selective reduction of a natural multiple pregnancy to ensure the growth of other pre-embryos or to preserve the life of the mother has always been acceptable. To deliberately implant a number of pre-embryos with a view to selectively reducing the weaker cannot be ethically acceptable. Yet another problem with possible international implications has arisen in America. We had a divorced couple wrangling in court over the custody of their frozen pre-embryos. The judge awarded temporary, whatever that might mean, custody to the woman stating that a pre-embryo was not the property of the couple and therefore not to be apportioned as such. Fortunately, this problem is unlikely to arise here as all our centres use a consent form signed by both partners as to the ultimate disposal of any frozen pre-embryos. But whether the pre-embryo can be regarded as the property of the couple or as a living being in its own right must be a matter for legislation in this country.

Donation of eggs by women who are to be sterilised raises a difficult problem and again one not yet covered by legislation. On the morning of the presentation of our fourth annual report to the press, there were stories circulating in some papers. These were to the effect that women who were awaiting sterilisation were being pressured to donate eggs. It was indicated that women on a long waiting list could jump the queue and be admitted to private hospitals if they agreed to be egg donors. It was also inferred that in some cases donors were being paid for the eggs thus donated. As you can imagine, the press seized on the opportunity of asking us as the Licensing Authority whether this was permitted under our licence. I explained that as an Authority this was a new issue which we had not yet discussed. However, we would hold a special meeting to try and reach a decision. The Warnock Committee recommended that the sale or purchase of human gametes or embryos should be permitted only under licence from and subject to conditions prescribed by the legislating body and any unauthorised sale or purchase should be made a criminal offence. We added the following addition to that recommendation and circulated the whole as a new guideline. We stated:

The Authority considers that any form of inducement to any woman to give eggs, such as the offer of free sterilisation, is equivalent to payment for gametes and is unacceptable. The Interim Licensing Authority is not prepared to license centres adopting this practice and furthermore it is assumed that once established, a Statutory Licensing Authority will make this a criminal offence. The Authority accepts that a number of women may wish to donate their eggs for purely altruistic reasons and this is quite acceptable provided that no inducement of any kind is offered and the patient receives adequate counselling about the risks of egg collection procedures and ovulation induction techniques. Donors should remain anonymous in line with the Authority's guidelines.

Following this circulation, we have had responses from some centres explaining methods of obtaining eggs from women to be sterilised and asking whether these are acceptable methods. This is a difficult ethical problem and we are in the process of trying to resolve what constitutes an improper inducement and what would be an acceptable one. There are so many ethical and other problems that arise for which legislation will go some way towards defining a solution, but over many there will always be controversy. I hope this controversy will not obscure what should be paramount in everybody's approach to this very delicate field of medicine — the future welfare of any child born by any means.

I do not believe that the formation of a Statutory Licensing Authority will solve the problem of the long waiting list for free or subsidised treatment. If, as has been suggested, the centres will have to pay a licence fee, I cannot foresee the National Health Service hospitals with their restricted budgets giving priority to infertility over life-threatening or crippling disease. I fear that it will still depend on your geographical location and the size of your pocket whether or not you receive treatment.

Finally, whatever legislation is forthcoming, as I have said there will always be ethical problems. Can one legislate for these? It depends in the

final analysis on the integrity and professional standards of those undertaking this work. This integrity and those standards have been maintained
by self regulation. All any legislation can do is to provide a legal framework
in which they can continue. Let us hope that the framework will not become
a restrictive cage whose bars prevent further and necessary research.

Index